I0094606

Rover

True stories of a dog

and his family

Other novels by Alfred Dennis

Chiricahua
Lone Eagle
Elkhorn Divide
Brant's Fort
Catamount
The Mustangers
Yuma
Yellowstone Divide
Sandigras Canyon
Shawnee Trail
Fort Reno

Rover

ALFRED DENNIS

WCP

Walnut Creek Publishing
Tuskahoma, Oklahoma

ROVER: True stories of a dog and his family

Copyright © 2012, 2014 by Alfred Dennis. All rights reserved.
No part of this publication may be reproduced, transmitted, or resold in whole
or in part in any form, without the express written permission of the author or publisher,
except for the use of brief quotations in a book review.

ISBN: 978-0-9893241-7-5
Second Edition, Paperback
Published 2014 by Walnut Creek Publishing
10 9 8 7 6 5 4 3 2

Books may be purchased in quantity and/or special sales by contacting the publisher;
Walnut Creek Publishing
PO Box 820
Talihina, OK 74571
www.wc-books.com

This book is dedicated to the Dennis Family, who lived, worked, and were a family down on the banks of Blue River, near Egypt, Oklahoma. Carl, Maybelle, Floyd, Reba, Wynona, Sylvia, Keith, RC, Herald Gene, and the youngest Joann.

Introduction

This is the story of a dog and the family he watched over, the dedication he gave them, and the hardships he encountered along the way. It is a true story, a remarkable, almost legendary story of Rover and the family he loved. There have been many canines in the movies but Rover was no movie dog; he was as they say, the real McCoy. This particular dog was one of a kind. He watched over a family, worked our cattle, hunted the meat for our table, and he was always there ready to listen to your problems when you were sad or troubled.

Rover was one of the most intelligent animals I have ever had the privilege of knowing. He was smart, loyal, and courageous but kind and gentle as well. I never knew him to start a fight, growl or bark at anyone or anything, well with the exception of a coon, bobcat or some other varmint. In his carriage, he was like an aristocrat of old, proud, honorable, the King of his domain.

Experts today tell us not to feed their animals table scraps but old Rover never ate anything except table leftovers. He mostly ate cornbread and biscuits, sometimes soaked with a little sweet milk, yet he lived to the ripe old age of sixteen, dying in nineteen hundred and sixty-two.

This is also the story of the farmer that raised him, taught him with patience and love, and was as loyal to the dog, as the dog was to him. It is also the story of a family, a family that did not have much as far as earthly things, money was scarce as hen's teeth back then but we were always blessed with plenty to eat. Down on the fertile black land farm they had one another and that is what really counts. Yes, this is a true story, a story of hardships, hard work, and loyalty to one another, the way it used to be.

There are not a lot of people alive now that knew old Rover when he was in his prime. There are still a few people that ask about the big red dog with the splash of white on his chest, the dog that belonged to Carl Dennis. I will guarantee you a smile comes to their faces as they remember those good old days.

He could run a coon down the river or tree a squirrel with the best of them. Cow dog or hog dog, Rover was as good as there was.

This story took place sixty years ago. The author of this story can go down to Egypt, Oklahoma to the old rock crossing on Blue River and still hear Carl's hounds running that old ring tail down the river. Go to Milburn, lots of folks there still remember the big reddish brown dog that fed his family, loved and protected them.

Eight miles east of Milburn, Oklahoma at the bend of the road stood the old one room Egypt Schoolhouse. Two miles farther along there is a crossroad. Turn north three quarters of a mile, look up to your left and you will see the old farmhouse of Carl Dennis and his family. The rough frame house sits on a small hill looking east down towards a large cornfield that nestles in the horseshoe shaped bottom of Blue River.

Carl Dennis and his sons farmed and hunted the bottoms along this once clear, clean little river. Back then, we bathed in Blue; we got our wash water by backing a team into the shallow water and filling up the barrels. The water was so clean and cool you could drink from it. On a hot summer afternoon, the clear water was mighty inviting. At night Carl and his family could sit on his front porch and hear the call of the whippoorwill or the sound of George Dunn's wolfhounds burning a track up. Back then only coal oil lamps lit the houses and only wood was used for heat and cooking. It was a hard life to some but not to Carl, he loved it. Hard work never hurt him, for he had his family and his beloved dogs.

Time passes, Carl and his good dogs Rover, Buck, Quane, Fanny, Ranger, and Rock are all gone now. However, the good times and memories will linger on in the author's mind and they will as long as he lives. It is a bygone day, days that were filled with happiness, few worries and great memories.

Most of the men that hunted with Rover or worked a cow with him are gone too but some remain who will remember.

Carl's wife Maybelle is gone now too but to any still living who remembers her she will forever be with us. She was one of a kind. She was a small woman with a big heart, full of love for her family. I never knew her to raise her voice but she did not have to. She never gave me but one strapping and I think it hurt her more than it did me. She was as gentle and kind as a fresh spring breeze. Yes, she was a small woman in statue but she had the heart of a giant. She could drive a team of horses hooked to a buck rake during hay season; she could milk a cow as fast as any man. Maybelle Dennis worked hard her whole life, her hands were rough, maybe even calloused but she was quite a lady. She raised seven children. One of her children, Herald Gene, was killed by an automobile between Milburn and Tishomingo across from the cemetery. It happened only a few feet from where he and his beloved folks, Carl and Maybelle, now rest.

Folks, this is the story of a dog and a family, and their times together way back when. Those days are long gone now and it is a shame, for it was a far better and quieter time. A time when people made their own way and depended only on their strong muscles and a good dog like Old Rover. I heard Pa say more than once. "A man can count his good fortunes if he has a good wife, a good gun, and a good dog." Well he had'em all, he was a fortunate man.

Chapter 1
Rover

The big farmer gazed into the dark barrel where a black and tan gyp licked and dried her newborn puppies. Smiling, he reached and picked up a wriggling male pup and his rough calloused hands stroked the small head. A white splash of hair covers the still wet chest. Putting the pup back, the man looks to where a collie sits curiously cocking his ears at the strange sounds coming from the barrel. Yep, Rover's mother was a black and tan hound, and his father a pureblood collie.

However, remember that was sixty years ago. Back then, farmers still plowed their fields with horses and made the trip to town on Saturday in wagons. Years before pedigrees counted but putting meat on the table did and that's what Rover did best. Only one pup was kept from the litter and that was the pup with the white splash. The first year, he had more than his fair share of problems, probably because he hung out with me. He was like me and he was full of deviltry and mischief. From running Granny's chickens, to pulling clothes off the clothesline, to busting through the milk cows, and scattering them everywhere, Old Rover was a terror alright. His natural curiosity kept him from missing out on anything happening around the farm and that's exactly what kept him in trouble most of the time. Carl had patience, it would take time but down on Blue there was plenty of that, he would let the pup mature before his real training would start. The time would come soon enough for Rover to go to work. He knew the pup was remarkably intelligent and with training, he knew Rover would make a good dog. Back in those days a sure 'nuff good dog was worth his weight in gold and the farmer knew the red dog was gonna be one of the best ever. It would take a gentle, patient hand and time, something the farmer had plenty of.

Six months pass, Rover's body grew and started to mature. Already my uncle RC bragged, he'd as soon take Rover to the woods after squirrels as the older hounds. Most times late in the day before sundown, when the chores were finished, we'd spend the hot summer evenings swimming in the river; running ahead Rover was always the first to get there. Now I didn't mind that because there was always a few water moccasins floating around the water's edge or lying coiled up asleep on the bank. Carl would always get a good-sized club and work them over but not RC, no sir; he'd just slip right in the water with them things and go swimming. Not me, I would sic Rover in to send them hightailing it for cover. I checked the sandy riverbanks and under every rock before I went in. Call me a chicken if you want but anybody knows a water moccasin can be a nasty little creature when riled. From the experiences I've had with the little devils they stay riled pert near all the time. No sir, I wasn't taking any chances on getting myself snake bit. Why I've had them slippery suckers come right out on the riverbank and chase me. RC said if I'd quit rocking the dat burned things and making them mad, they'd leave me alone. I didn't believe him; I had me a better remedy. A well-aimed rock right twixt their beady little eyeballs was better, I always believed anything human or varmint respected a well-placed rock. I've beaned me a many of them things but all they did was pull their nasty heads back and stick out their tongues. Only reason I figured RC got along with them things was, shucks he was meaner than they were. Our other pastime was coon hunting and it was my favorite way to spend an evening. The early dusky dark was when the woods would come alive, yet it was also serene and peaceful. Carl Dennis was a hardworking farmer at heart but his one great love, besides Granny that is, was coon hunting. He knew all about coon hunting and he loved a good coon dog. Yes sir, he really enjoyed a good coon race.

The whole family would sit by the fire on a cold freezing night after the chores were finished; eating hot poached peanuts and listen to him tell bygone stories of rugged hunters, coon hunts, and dogs. Yes sir, Pa could sure tell a yarn, you'd listen to his soft voice spinning a tale and you could picture yourself right there. His stories were so real you could even smell the wet dogs and the coon. I would sit there looking at the red-hot fire and picture it all in my mind. Somehow, he could make them come alive. I swear listening to Pa, you could actually hear those hounds bawling on a hot track.

He also loved a good stock dog and in Rover, he had the best of both breeds. Anyone knows training a stock dog is much more difficult than training a hunting dog. A hound just naturally is gonna run anything they smell or see, in front of them and sometimes that creates a little problem. Most hunters don't want their dogs running trash, which includes possums, armadillos, deer, rabbits, and such.

Now down on Blue River we didn't have deer, so that solved that problem but we had plenty of possum and rabbits to go around. Some hunters were strictly meat hunters and they didn't care what their dogs ran. Not Carl, no sir, his dogs better run a straight coon track and nothing else or there was gonna be hades to pay. Most times hunters always had an older dog ahead of them to help train the younger pups and we did for coon or squirrel hunting. Pa had a little red bone gyp named Quane, the best coonhound outside of Rover I ever knew and he had a black and tan named Fanny.

Training Rover to work cattle would be a harder job as Carl didn't have an older dog to train him with. As Rover grew and matured, Carl would walk the big red pup to the crossing every night to bring in the cows for milking. The farmer would cross the river with Rover roaming ahead and together they'd go find the cows. Most of the time Blue River was low and the river could be crossed easily on the protruding rocks. Driving the cows back across slow and easy Carl would hiss the pup hollering the old familiar word "huh ee". Don't reckon I ever heard anyone but us use the term, most of our neighbors only hollered sic'em or get'em. The farmer would speak to Rover who would tilt his head and look back and forth between him and the cows, not knowing exactly what the farmer wanted.

It didn't take long though, like I said, Rover was intelligent and he was a quick learner. I always remembered Rover had a quiet almost aristocratic look about him. I've found through the years, all good dogs, whatever they were trained for had that look and carriage. Proud, intelligent, and confident in themselves, they seem to walk with pride.

Rover finally figured out that pushing the cows up the lane to the stomp was a lot of fun. He could bark and move them cows without being scolded, like Granny would do if she caught him running her prize-laying hens. There he would lie down and watch as Carl and his youngest son RC would turn a calf in with its mother and start milking. RC always enjoyed squirting a little milk over at the dog that is if he could do so without getting caught. Pa didn't like to see anything wasted. Living through the great depression, I reckon it caused him to be very thrifty where food was concerned. I've heard the older folks speak of them days and it sure must have been rough. I've heard Granny say, there were many times when folks would stop by to visit and all they had was raw potatoes to eat with not even grease to fry them in. Still, meager as the meal was, nobody left her house hungry back then or later when times were better.

Those long ago summer nights down on Blue were peaceful and quiet. They didn't have television or telephones back then, just cards or dominoes to pass the time. Shucks, we didn't even have electricity. Most nights after our chores were finished, when we weren't hunting or swimming, there would be a hot domino game going, on the front porch with just a dim coal oil lantern to light the table. A number three washtub, half-full of water, was kept close under the light to catch the bugs that flew carelessly into it. Pa sure didn't let us waste coal or oil, kerosene as it is called now. The only time the lamps were lit was when we were doing our homework or a good domino or pitch game was going on.

I loved to watch the games being played but there was one thing that always amazed me. If Joann and RC were playing against Granny and Pa which they normally did, lo and behold, when the game started RC and Joann would always have their shoes on. However, if they started losing, why them shoes would come off slicker than a peeled onion. Now I ain't saying there was any cheating going on, no sir. I don't want them peeling my head. Most times, it was hot out there on the porch and probably their feet needed cooling off so they just naturally removed their shoes. One thing I did notice under that table, their toes were touching and they seemed to be tapping out some kind of code or something.

Pa and Granny were honest to a fault but RC and Joann, well let me say, when it came to a pitch game or a domino game they were going to win, one way or the other. Course now, even today they'd deny any unscrupulous playing and I ain't saying they would out and out cheat, just let me say they were a little devious in their game playing. I reckon it was all in fun and harmless, many a night was passed laughing and pounding on that old table. Some don't remember but Pa would always holler "bluey" when he made a good score. His head would roll back and he'd let out with that deep laugh of his causing his stomach to bounce up and down.

Rover was a year past and he was beginning to work cows like a bona fide cow dog. Now this tickled RC as it was his job to get the cows up every morning and evening for milking. We always kept either the cows lotted or their calves so most of the time one or the other would be waiting at the milk lot but occasionally RC would have to cross Blue and point them crafty old cows towards home. I can't blame them old mama cows for not wanting to come in. Their calves were fat and sassy and the way they latched on their mama's udders for more milk had to hurt.

Now this weren't always in the summer months, the cows needed milking in the winter same as summer. You ever tried walking a half-mile or more in the dark or in the cold winter? It ain't exactly fun, cause, come rain, sleet, snow, or shine, those old cows had to be milked. RC would have to cross that river no matter what, shucks I've seen him break ice and swim Blue River more than once. I felt kinda sorry for him but not sorry enough to hit that water alongside him. I just couldn't see where two of us were needed to handle a few old gentle milk cows, no sir; my mama didn't raise an idiot.

That's where Rover came in. With Carl or RC bringing up the cows every day, the big dog, day by day, ventured a little farther and then even farther. Then the day finally came when all Carl had to do was holler Rover "huh ee" and he'd be off like a shot after the herd.

He wouldn't push them hard. He just let them old cows walk at their own pace back to the stomp lot. Many days, I stood at the river crossing and watched him actually smell of each cow, almost like he was counting them. Next thing I knew he'd head back for the one that was missing. Pa always said the only thing he couldn't teach old Rover was to bring the horses in first if he wanted them. The big red dog always brought the cattle first and then he'd go back after the horses.

I know a lot of stockmen nowadays that don't like to work their horses with a dog. They think it'll make a horse learn to kick or hard to catch. Plus a horse's hoof is mighty rough on a dog's head, should they connect. Not old Rover, I never knew him to get kicked and I've seen more than one try. I've seen a few stubborn old mules when they first arrived at the farm try to outrun him or bluff him but like the man said in the song, they got themselves an attitude adjustment. After a few days on the farm, if they were within earshot when they heard Carl holler Rover "huh ee", they'd head for the stomp lot calm as lambs. I wouldn't doubt if it had been possible, they would have tried to put their own harness on.

Rover was always ready and on the alert. He watched over all the proceedings while our chores were being done. He never let his vigilance down until the last bucket of milk left for the house. Then he would head for his favorite place on the porch. I've had a whole passel of dogs and some really good ones but Rover stood head and shoulders above them all. Plus, he was the most loyal one of all. He was a real working dog but more than that, he was a trusted friend.

Chapter 2
Roy Dobbs and the Bull

It was a typical hot spring day. Needing a seed bull, Pa hitched a ride to the Durant Sale Barn with our neighbor George Dunn. Pa was looking to purchase himself a sure enough good Hereford bull, providing one passed through the sale ring that day. Pa's bull buying escapade all started when some cattle buyers from Texas were traveling around the county buying up yearlings and anything else they could make a profit on.

Days before they put out the word that they would be traveling through our part of the county and advertised anyone with yearling bulls or steers for sale were to leave word with Murk's Mercantile Store in Milburn. Hearing of the buyers, Pa sent word by our letter carrier C.B. Houser to Mister Murk that he had six good yearling steers ready to go. True to their word, the cattle buyers promptly sent word back that they'd be at our farm the next Monday but they didn't say what time. Pa had work to do cultivating his cornfield to keep the Johnson grass from taking over, so he left RC sitting up at the milk lot waiting for them. Course now, as I wasn't much use to help with the plowing I was content to wait right there and help RC and Rover bring in the cows. Like I said, RC my uncle was older than I was. I always wanted to be wherever he was, unless he was mad at me about something. Course now, I can't say he treasured my company all that much. I could be a pest most of the time, talked too much I reckon.

"Now boy, I ain't gonna keep my stock in a dry lot all day in hopes these city folks are gonna show. When and if those buyers get here, you send Rover after the cows and lot those six yearlings."

"Yes Sir."

Pa reached inside his shirt, pulled out a wrinkled handwritten bill of sale, and handed it to RC "They'll give you two hundred dollars, you give them this paper."

"Yes Sir." RC wasn't long-winded; he sure wasn't about to waste much time with words.

Soon as Pa walked away driving his team ahead of him, we pulled us up a spot of shade under the old bois d'arc tree out front of the house. Leaning back against the tree, we made ourselves comfortable and speculated on when or if the buyers would arrive. RC bet they'd get to our farm alright but I figured they'd probably get themselves lost. Back then, there weren't too many road signs and matter of fact there weren't any signs at all on our dirt roads. There were lots of dirt roads that is if you want to call them roads.

"Bet you ten marbles, they'll show."

I kinda balked at that idea. Marbles were hard to come by then, even though every kid had a pocketful. We played keepsies all the way to school, during school, and after school. Many a good marble games were finished with a black eye or bloody nose and most times, I was on the receiving end, of the black eyes that is.

They were city dudes we were dealing with and I could sure use ten more marbles. As of late, I had been getting clipped pretty good after school and my marbles were getting about as scarce as whiskers on a rooster. "Alright, I'll bet." My big mouth popped open knowing full well RC seldom lost a bet. Matter of fact, come to think of it, I don't ever remember too many people getting the best of him on any bet he ever made. Kinda like the domino or card games, he was tricky.

I knew it, I should have known better than to make that bet. Shucks we hadn't even nodded to seal the bet when RC grinned. He could hear the sound of their truck coming and I could see my marbles slipping into his pocket. I sat there listening to that old truck coming up the road and cussed my foolhardiness. I swore right then never to bet with him again. However, my swearing off of anything never lasted long; I was just a sucker for a bet. Whether it be marbles, cards, or even seeing who could spit the farthest. No sir, I weren't scared to wager on anything but sometimes I sure could be dumber than a box of rocks.

The big truck trimmed with high side boards huffed, puffed, and rattled up the hill. Pulling up near where we sat, it shuttered to a stop, backfired once and went silent. Two men sat in the front of that big truck staring down and grinning at us two barefooted country boys. I swear those men were huge and their hats were even bigger. I reckoned I had never seen a truck near as big as the one they were in. Back then, we didn't see a dozen trucks a year come to our farm and most of them were lost when they did manage to wind up in our yard.

"Is this the Carl Dennis Farm?"

"Yes Sir." RC looked over at the old plank house and nodded. "What's left of it."

I didn't know if my neck was gonna bend far enough back to look up at the man as he unlimbered himself from that seat. I swear back then I thought he had to have been ten feet tall. Now I know better, it was probably closer to eight feet; no matter, he was a big 'un. Shoot, if he hadn't of been so bowlegged, he'd probably would have been a ten footer.

"We got word in town you have some yearlings for sale." The driver rolled out the words in a long Texas drawl, the likes of which I never heard before. "We're cattle buyers."

"Yes Sir, my Pa does." Now I always thought RC was tall or at least it felt that way when he was mad and smacking me around. Next to these men, he seemed awful small, kinda like that midget I seen once at a carnival in town.

"Well, we've come to look'em over."

"Yes Sir, Dad's in the field down yonder." RC poked his chin out towards the lower field. "He told me to get'em up for you."

RC looked over to where Rover was watching the proceedings then hollered "huh ee" and the big red dog was gone. I watched as the men's eyes kinda focused and grew narrow, watching as Rover disappeared from sight.

"That red dog gonna bring your cows in?"

"He's supposed to." RC seemed a little put out that they'd ask such a fool question. He sure wasn't sending Rover to the river to pick flowers. "You men like a cold drink of water?"

"No thank ye son, how long you 'spect it'll take him?" The taller of the men acted as if he was doubtful to me. The other one kept fidgeting like his feet were itching or something.

"Not long." RC was crisp and to the point with the men, which wasn't anything new. He was that way with most people. He sure wasn't the friendliest or most talkative feller I ever met. Most times, he acted like it was hurting him to talk at all.

I watched as one of the men fished a Bull Durham sack from his shirt pocket and rolled himself a cigarette. I swear, quicker than a cat could lick up cream in a saucer, he rolled that tobacco, licked the paper once, twirled it in his fingers, and struck a match on his denim jeans. I had to admit, it sure smelled a lot better to me than the old hollow vines we puffed on from time to time.

Occasionally, we'd touch off a cigarette butt out of the ones we picked up on the street in town. Pa always had us gather up what butts we could find laying about on the street; he said it would worm out our horses. Now I know he didn't mean for us to try them ourselves but I figured whatever was good for the horses should be good for me. Of course, now the horses weren't smoking the things.

Well the man hardly finished his smoke, crunching it out under his fine high heeled boots, when Rover came pushing the cattle up the lane. The milk cows were in the lead with the yearlings bucking and playing behind them. I slipped past the herd and closed the barbwire gate to keep their devious little minds from considering escaping back to the cool bottoms of the river. Course now their best efforts at freedom were always foiled. They tried that several times before and they learned long ago better not try to outsmart the big dog.

The old cows stood around bunched in a corner looking bored, as RC would point to a yearling he wanted then Rover would slowly work him into the lot, where I promptly shut the gate. Not a sound came from the red dog as he loaded all six steers without stirring up the other cattle. He just eased up to whichever one he wanted, pointed that yearling in the right direction and into the smaller lot he went. I was proud of Old Rover that day, showing his stuff in front of them Texans. I figured they had never seen a dog like him.

"Load that bull, boy."

"Dad don't aim to sell him." RC stared over to where the men stood beside the fence.

"I know, we just want to see the dog work him."

Shrugging, RC pointed at the bull and I opened the gate. Slick as a peeled onion Rover added the bull in with the rest of the younger stock then plopped himself down in the gate, guarding against any attempted escapes. Well right then and there, I noticed something kinda peculiar about this deal. The Texans hadn't paid the slightest attention to them big fat yearlings, no sir; they had their eyes glued on Rover. It kinda reminded me of the way a fox looked at a chicken, you know, kinda hungry like. Not that any of the cattle put up a fight, it was the calm way he lotted the calves and bull that struck their fancy. Shucks, Rover was so smooth; he didn't even stir up the swarm of flies sitting atop their backs.

"How much you want for the dog, young man?" One of the men stuck his overgrown chin out towards Rover. I kinda liked him calling RC young man. RC wouldn't take much off anybody except Pa and I could tell he was getting a mite perturbed. Messing with him was kinda like messing with dynamite, it didn't take much to set his temper off.

"Rover? Shucks mister that dog ain't for sale." RC sounded shocked they would even venture such an idea.

"One hundred dollars!" The man whipped out a roll of bills that would have choked an elephant, not that I had seen too many of them varmints. I had seen them in books and their mouths looked pretty big.

"He ain't for sale." RC assured the men. Now I don't know if my uncle loved that dog or it might just have been he hated hitting that cold river every morning after the cows. I'm just glad I wasn't big enough yet or he'd of been sending me after them, the same way he did poor Old Rover. I was growing; day by day, I was getting there. Thought maybe I would quit eating and stunt my growth a little, you know stave off the inevitable.

I had to admit them Texans were persistent cusses. They sure didn't take no for an answer. "Tell you what; I'll give two hundred for him."

"Mister, that dog belongs to my Dad and he's down there in that field plowing. Now, it ain't about to do you no good but I see you're a man that don't take no for an answer." RC pointed off down the hill to where Pa was running a cultivator through the rows of corn. "You want him all that bad, you'll have to go down there but I'm telling you, you're wasting your time. There ain't enough money made to buy him, he'd rather sell one of us than Rover."

Well that's exactly what they did, cowboy boots, big hats, bowlegs, and all. I looked over at RC and I could tell exactly what he was thinking. Now I've never known RC to speak bad about any man and you sure didn't talk about a woman in front of him, even when he was a youngster. All the same, I could tell what he was thinking. Me, I didn't mind talking about anybody. It got me a few black eyes but I was kinda like that elephant, I had a big mouth.

Well we returned to the shady spot under the old bois d'arc tree and watched the proceedings. Walking all the way, down to where Pa was plowing was about as useless as pouring water down a red ant bed hoping to drown them out. I sure up and learned that the hard way. Once long before I became educated, I poured three full buckets of water down a red ant hole and got exactly one ant to come out. He weren't drowned either but he bit the snot out of me when I was stupid enough to pick him up.

Sure enough, it weren't long before those fellers came huffing and puffing back up the hill. All hot and red faced, they seemed a little agitated and had completely forgotten about the six yearlings. Weren't no need in asking what kind of answer they got, I could tell that by the frowns on their faces. Rover sure wasn't gonna be leaving with them.

"You fellers ain't taking the steers?" RC already knew the answer to that one but he just had to have his fun.

Only a glare came from the men as they heaved their big selves into the cab of that truck and roared back down the drive with every hound on the place chasing and bellowing behind them. I could kinda tell from the way they were blowing when they got back to us that they weren't just real fond of walking. I always had heard a real Texas cowboy would ride a horse five feet to a gate before he'd walk and lead his horse to one. They sure had their pride, walking anywhere just wasn't the cowboy thing to do. Around this part of the country we call that lazy but I wasn't about to say anything.

Well we sat there contemplating what we were gonna do with the cows when Rover whined and wagged his tail. Pa came walking up and gave us the once over which normally meant we had better find something to do and mighty quick. Looking down the lane to where the dust was beginning to settle he shook his head and nodded at the corral. "Turn 'em out, we got work to do."

Walking to the gate, I was just about to spring the latch when here came that truck again just a roaring up the hill. Pa kinda stood there his eyes a blinking, then I saw the hint of a grin come over his face. Well, have you ever seen a possum grin down at you from a tree limb? That's exactly what he looked like alright. I knew right then, those Texans were about to pay a little more money than they intended for them six calves. That big truck sputtered and shook a time or two, belched out a puff of smoke then came to a halt in exactly the same spot they stopped earlier.

Yep, I was right, Pa sold the six steers to them Texans, it took a little hem hawing around and a little horse-trading but he got a little extra for them. After all, he had to walk all the way to the house to tell us how to open a gate to turn them steers out and a man's time in the morning heat, now that should be worth something.

Right about then is where Roy Dobbs and the little Hereford Bull
came into the picture. It seems our Texas buyers guaranteed they'd be
back next year providing Pa got himself a good Hereford Bull, not the
scrawny mix blood that was standing all humped up in the truck with
them yearlings.

Sure enough, Pa sold his bull to them Texans, shucks might as well,
it was already in the corral and the dang thing was kinda scrawny to
boot. Anyhoo now he had money in his pocket to buy a good bull. That
week off he went to Durant and found himself a real nice little old
horned Hereford. Next, he up and hired Roy Dobbs, a stock buyer to
deliver the bull that same afternoon. It was after dinner, Pa was standing
out in the yard eagerly awaiting Mister Dobb's and our new bull to
arrive. The rest of the family stood about the yard, along with a
menagerie of dogs, chickens, and a stray cat or two. Every eye was fixed
on Mister Dobb's old truck as it came rolling up the lane and backed up
screeching to a halt in front of our best number one, foolproof, mule
holding corral, leastways at the time I thought it was foolproof.

Me and RC put our hoes down and meandered over to see our new
arrival that stood all alone, huddled in the rear of that truck. Any excuse
to be out of the garden suited me just fine. Man, you talk about slave
labor, that was us alright but with Granny's good cooking, we sure ate
like kings. Now, my critical cowman's eye was a little bit dubious to say
the least as I looked through the slats of the truck's side boards at the
new addition to the farm.

At first glimpse, the bull didn't seem to be in too good a mood.
When I got a little too close, he up and hooked one of those oak boards
cracking it into kindling. Retreating to a better or should I say safer place
to watch the show, I was all eyes as Mister Dobbs jerked the tailgate
loose and let that Hereford out. Maybe I should clarify that and say he
turned a tornado loose right in the middle of our best corral or what was
a corral. The little bull went through them poles like syrup through a
pancake. My eyes were all bugged out in shock and disbelief with my
mouth dropped open, man what a show that Hereford put on. That
sucker pawed and hooked the ground then whirled around and gave me

a nasty look. That was enough to convince me to find a safer place higher on what was left of the fence to watch the proceedings.

What happened next was kinda funny though, leastways after I finally settled myself out of harms way in a safer place to observe the situation. That Hereford scattered spectators, dogs, and chickens. I mean everything started looking for greener pastures as he passed through what was left of our corral, pawing and a hooking the ground, throwing dirt everywhere. That bull never looked back or hesitated as he took our barbwire fence with him when he hit the sandy lane, headed for the county road. Like the man said, he was headed west and I for one was glad to see him vacate the premises.

Mister Roy Dobbs was a bona fide horse and cattle trader and that meant he could talk himself out of or into any situation. I've never seen the man at a loss for words before but this time he was speechless and dumbstruck. He was standing there with his jaw opening and closing like a screen door without a spring. Now you have to remember, Mister Dobbs made his living buying, selling, and delivering critters to and from the local farms. This wasn't gonna look good on his unblemished record, especially with all the eyewitnesses to talk of it. Mainly me, everybody in these parts knew I was a blabbermouth for sure, which made me a perfect witness, I never missed a thing.

"Carl." I swear Mister Dobbs stammered the word at least four times before his tongue came loose and started to work. "Carl, get me a horse and I'll get him back, better yet I'll give you your money back."

Pa just laughed, he had never seen Mister Dobbs shocked into being so generous before. "Don't worry about it Roy, he ain't going nowhere."

Well, I don't know but it looked to me like that little old bull was already gone. I blinked again and looked around, our corrals and yard looked like a cyclone done up and passed through it. I had to admit; while it lasted, it was quite a show, a lot more exciting than the carnival we went to last year.

"I reckon we had that Hereford a mite stirred up when we finally got him loaded." Roy removed his hat and scratched his baldhead. "I sure figured he would have settled down by now."

Rover was standing beside Pa watching intently as the Hereford trotted out of sight and started for the crossroads headed for parts unknown. I had to admit that little bull was a looker. Square, slab-sided, straight-backed, with heavy legs, and he had a small head for easy calving, yes sir he was a dandy. The big dog stood there unconcerned as Pa patted him on the head, then pointed and hollered "huh ee".

"Carl, I don't think that dog will get your bull back all by himself, stirred up like he is." Roy shook his head. "I'd dang near bet on it; you better get me a horse." Now my Grandpa wasn't a betting man but I could see by the look in his eye that he was sorely tempted this time. Anybody criticizing Old Rover's abilities could sure get the big farmer's ire and get it quick. Not RC, he was a different breed of fish altogether. He'd bet the outcome of anything if he thought it was worth his time and what made it so bad he almost always won. However, this time he kept quiet, although I knew he was chomping at the bits wanting to con Mister Dobbs into this bet.

"Roy, it'll be alright, that bull will be back pretty quick." Pa kinda smiled. "I'll guarantee it."

"Well Carl, if you don't mind, I've got me a notion to sit right here. I want to see this for myself." At that, all of us pulled up a spot of shade and listened to the fight going on down the road as Mister Dobbs continued to look towards the noise. "I feel responsible. I ain't leaving until I see that bull safe back home and I'm paying you for the damage he done to your place."

I don't think he was so worried about the bull getting back safe, no sir; Mister Dobbs just wanted to see if Rover could bring the Hereford back by himself. I got to hand it to that little bull though, he was tough. We sat there almost two hours listening to Mister Dobbs horse stories and bad cattle tales. Finally, the Hereford came trotting back around the bend up to the stomp lot, with Old Rover trotting along a few feet behind him. Now I have to admit, he weren't near as pretty as he once was. Most bulls have two ears and a nose that's not tore up. Rover did bring him back alive, kinda like on radio when the Lone Ranger brought his prisoner in a little worse for wear, but alive.

I reckon that's how Rover's reputation got started because Roy Dobbs liked to talk, almost as much as I did, every time he told the story the bull got bigger and the day got hotter. Why, we've had people come to the farm to see what this giant bull looked like only to leave in pure disappointment at the sight of our one-eared, little old Hereford. What's worse, we ain't seen nary hide nor hair of them Texas Cattle buyers to this day. Let that be a lesson to you, don't ever trust a Texan. I got to admit, Rover put on a show that day that probably made him famous, at least it earned him the title of cow dog. I guess by the time Mister Dobbs was finished spreading his yarns, everybody in Johnston County knew of Old Rover.

Chapter 3
The Coon Hunters

Well things kinda quieted down around the old farm after the bull incident. Summer was on us hot and heavy, I found myself continually looking out the window of the one room schoolhouse and dreaming of the woods. I ain't never figured out why they named this corner of the world Egypt but that was its name sure enough. I did learn in school there was a country far away in the old world called Egypt but a schoolhouse on a small dirt road in nowhere Oklahoma, well that took the cake. Even our schoolteacher Almond Rowland who we all thought was the greatest and smartest schoolteacher ever, didn't quite know the answer to that one. He said it was named Egypt schoolhouse long before my Grandfather ever gave him his first teaching job. At that time, the big farmer was also president of the school board. I did know one thing for certain; I did more daydreaming out that open window than I did book learning. You see back then paper wasn't too plentiful so we used the old blackboard, plus our memory to study with. The way I figured it, there wasn't any use for my eyes and ears both being used for learning, so my ears listened to the lessons and my eyes daydreamed out the window. Some people would say that weren't possible but I got it done sure'nuff. I didn't make near the grades Joann did but I managed to get myself passed on to the next grade.

Most kids in the big cities are out of school during the summer months but not us. No Sir, we were lucky, we got to go to school during the heat of summer so we could save up our energy for the fall harvest, then the spring planting. You see the school board and government knew back then that parents bossed us kids, weren't nothing like today, if we were needed to work we would be kept home. I could just imagine what would have happened back then if the government told my folks I was going to do what they said, not what my parents said. Our folks, they sure didn't have all us kids around to decorate the house.

The jest of it was we were out of school in the spring to work the fields and then out in the fall to harvest the crops. In short, we went to school to rest. Shoot, most kids except me enjoyed school. Our little old school had one room and eight grades. Just imagine sitting through eight years of the same lessons being recited day after day. Now I never pretended to be a genius, no sir, but even an idiot has to learn something in that kind of environment. Like I said, Almond was a good teacher. He drummed stuff into my little old brain that I ain't forgot today and when I was bad, he'd drum my backsides too.

Some days at school were better, like the time all the older boys got licks at school and to my amusement RC collected some of them. I wasn't too amused after school when he got through with me but at the time as I was leaning out the window, watching with some of the other younger boys and it was downright funny. In Egypt School House if you needed to go to the outhouse, you signed your name on the blackboard and went outside. Egypt didn't have a whole lot of kids in that little old school and very few were older boys. Just imagine Almond looking out over his flock and lo and behold all the bigger boys were missing. Their seats were as empty as a water bucket full of holes.

It sure didn't take much figuring to come to the conclusion that something was amiss. I watched full of anticipation as Almond looked over at the blackboard then at the empty seats. He stood up and walked slowly from the room with a hard scowl on his face. Course now us smaller kids being ate up with curiosity rushed to the window to watch the fireworks. You see we knew what the older boys were up to, this was gonna be a good show, as they said back then, a humdinger. Well durn it, we didn't get to watch but we could sure hear. Our schoolteacher caught his prize pupils right in the middle of a tobacco class, well maybe a smoking class. Every time that board hit, we could hear them poor souls moan. Shucks I even moaned, I could feel them licks myself, those hard whacks made your backsides kinda draw up just thinking about that wood paddle.

I do believe that paddling surpassed the skunk incident last winter when one of the smaller boys, I won't mention who, put a skunk's dead body in the old wood stove under the kindling. When that fire caught on and started roasting our smelly little friend, well let me tell you, we dang near froze to death with the windows wide open in the dead of winter, trying to air that schoolhouse out. What a smell, skunk is bad enough but roasted skunk whew-ee it smelled. It was downright funny to tell about, especially watching the girls hold their noses and squirming around in their seats. Even after the paddling all of us boys got when no one in particular would own up to doing the grizzly deed, it was still funny. I don't reckon Almond ever did find out who the culprit was but naturally, everyone blamed poor little old innocent me. Oh yea, I got my fair share of licks, plus several of the older boys tried to rearrange my nose a time or two after school let out. Naturally, I proclaimed my innocence for all to hear which didn't help my nose or backside any though.

Well summer was on us sure enough. One evening when we finished in the milk lot, I was gathering firewood to fill up the wood box for the kitchen when I heard the unmistakable sound of a car coming up the lane. I had my neck all craned out as far as it would reach when around the corner came two men in what they called a jeep. Pulling to a stop, among the growling and bawling of our hounds, the two men looked at us like I would have looked at superman, if he was right smack-dab in our front yard.

Now I'll grant you we were definitely country, Pa always wore bib overalls and us boys were dressed only in blue jeans. Shoes were not optional in the summertime unless you were going to school or Sunday go to meeting. They sure were looking long and hard at us but we were gawking at them too. Before us, stood bona fide city folks and they were duded up like they were headed for a funeral or something. They smelled like a cross between a rosebush and a cinnamon sprig.

Dismounting from that shiny jeep, a big likable grin plastered all over his face, the driver stuck out his hand and introduced himself. "We're looking for the Carl Dennis farm."

"Well son, you found it." Pa wrapped his big hand around the man's own. "I'm Carl Dennis, now what exactly can we do fer you?"

The city slicker introduced his partner who just rounded the jeep tiptoeing his way through our hounds. "Mister Dennis, we were told in town you had the best coon hunting in the country. Blue Bottom, I believed they call it."

"And you're coon hunters." Pa glanced at the box in the back of the jeep. We had already heard the whining and movement of dogs coming from it.

"We are Sir, name's Tim Mears and this is my brother Jackie Joe. We have some coon dogs with us. The best Walkers money can buy."

Now Pa's ears came on point. Coon hunting was his shortfall, he loved it and he loved his dogs. Now Pa wasn't lazy no sir, weren't a lazy bone in his body. When he had his choice between a good domino game or a coon hunt, he'd let the crops grow up in Johnson grass, he just had to go. His way of thinking was he had just been challenged. Him being a sure 'nuff sportsman who loved his dogs, he just couldn't, in no way, let the challenge from this city slicker slide. "Yes Sir, we do have some good hunting in these parts."

"Well then, would you mind if we hunted here tonight?" The young man smiled innocently.

Now, I ain't no idiot, his bubbling innocence was the same technique I always used to get what I wanted when I was a wanting something real terribly bad. Nope, I figured right, he was leading up to something.

"You boys are welcome to hunt all you want, the rivers just north and east of us."

"Well, we were hoping maybe you'd go with us and bring your good dogs we've heard so much about." The two men smiled at each other slyly. "We wouldn't want to get lost or anything."

There it was, I had already seen the once over's they were giving our pot lickers. Them city slickers were a wanting to run their Walker's against Pa's hounds. Now it's a fact Pa's dogs looked like nine miles of bad roads. Thin as newspapers and scarred all over from briars and thorns. They weren't just real pretty, matter of fact they were downright ugly. What our city dudes didn't look at was the underlying muscle these dogs had from running hard almost every night and the bright shine in their eyes. Pa's dogs were well fed, maybe not with the bagged dog food that these rich folks had but they were fed and they were healthy. Now, I don't think these men took in their finer points at all. I figure, but remember now mind you, I was just a young whippersnapper and according to some, downright ignorant when it came to most things. Anyway, I figured these boys were in for a lesson on the finer points of coon hunting. Yep, those city boys were already licking their lips, their mouths watering in anticipation of running their hounds against Pa's.

"Gentlemen, supper is on the table, ya'll come on in and we'll discuss our upcoming hunt." Pa smiled his biggest and navigated them city dudes through our pack of hounds towards the house. "You mind if we unload our dogs?"

I had to admit when those dogs came out of that box my eyes got big as saucers. Even RC was impressed and it took a lot to impress that boy. I had never seen dogs as pretty or as big as them two hounds. They had ears that hung at least an inch below their nose. I wondered how they could run a track without stepping on them but man, they were pretty.

"They're Walker Hounds, fastest dogs running a track on four feet." The driver threw out his chest, watching as I admired the Walkers.

"Well they are sure pretty, that's a fact." Pa agreed, looking the dogs over; he truly admired a good dog or really any dog that was worth his salt.

I was convinced. I could hardly eat a bite of my supper. I was so eager to get into the woods and watch them hounds work. I knew I was fixing to see the eighth wonder of the world, I just knew it, man was I excited. I kept glancing out the window to where those dogs were tied. I never knew supper to take so long. Now my Granny, she was a great cook, I ain't disputing that fact but man I was aching to get going and fast. What was taking that food so long to cook? Course now it would probably help if it was dark, which it wasn't. I was just gonna have to wait a spell.

After supper, me and RC started filling up our carbide lights and coal oil lanterns. Our new found friends had the newfangled lights that could throw a light fifty feet or better. Course now they would also shine brighter and that was the problem. Most times, old Mister Coon didn't like to look down at a real bright light. Now on the other hand, they weren't near as smelly or messy as our carbide lights or the coal oil lantern.

Yep, those electric lights were great but a little newfangled for me, shucks we didn't even have electric lights in the house. Supper was finally over and us coon hunters retreated to the porch to talk dogs and wait on the coming dark. At the time, I was still young and impressionable and them black and white Walker Hounds with a splash of brown here and there were the prettiest things I ever saw since Molly Andrews came to school. Course now, she was just a girl so she didn't really count, not like a good dog.

I knew Pa had shown time and again that his dogs were the best in Johnston County and anybody who had ever hunted with Rover, Quane, or Fanny would testify to that. Course now those dogs were raised in Blue Bottom. They learned to hunt squirrel and coon along the creek banks. I definitely believe they were on first name basis with most of the critters running the river. If they weren't, they should be as much as we hunted them, yep our dogs they had the advantage alright. Rover and Pa's other dogs ran them critters so much we knew what they were fixing to do before they did.

I was standing near the Walker dogs, studying them closely,

admiration dripping from my eyes. I felt almost like a traitor to Pa and his dogs cause I was figuring these magnificent animals were gonna run our dogs clean out of the bottoms tonight.

"Boy, you like those Walkers?" One of the young men slipped up silently beside me, as I was oohing and ahhing myself into a dither.

"Yes Sir, I do." I was always taught to say yes sir or no sir, and some of that teaching had been taught hard with a good strap. "They sure are pretty."

"Yes, they are for a fact." The man watched my eyes as they went from one dog to another. "I've never seen prettier."

"I 'spect they cost quite a bit?"

"Yes, they did. How do you think they'll do against your grandpa's dogs?"

"Well Sir, they'll have their hands full, I 'spect."

"So I've been told." The man grinned down at me. "But, I'll tell you what, you stick with me tonight and they'll show you how to tree a coon."

"Yes Sir."

"Another thing, next time I'm in this country, I'm gonna bring you one of these Walker pups. How'd you like that?"

"Gosh." Was all I could muster at the time, as I was already hunting the bottoms with that pup.

The man walked off as RC ambled over. He cold eyed the Walkers and looked about the same at me. "Looks of them hounds, all they've ever run is a dinner plate."

It was a fact, their dogs were fatter than ours but that wasn't anything. Our dogs standing sideways could pass for razor blades. Still, knowing this, I resented RC bringing it to my attention.

"Betcha ten marbles them pot lickers fall out of the first race." RC knew dogs and he knew the bottoms were hot and muggy this time of year. He was betting the fat those Walkers were carrying would be their downfall.

There was the old marble bet again. I hated not to back them pretty Walker dogs but I learned a long time ago not to bet against RC as he seldom lost. I figured several times he missed his calling, should have been one of those card sharks I'd heard about. He might have been too, in one of them earlier lives they taught us about in school, reincarnation or something like that. As lucky and ornery as he was sometimes, he might even have been one of those riverboat gamblers.

I felt like a rat abandoning a sinking ship as I looked into them Walkers eyes but I worked and fought hard for them marbles and I wasn't about to lose them. "Nope."

"Well then, pull your eyes back in your head and let's go." RC turned and walked away.

We started down the lane to the river. Pa only brought Rover and Quane making it a four-dog race. Quane was a small Redbone gyp, probably one of the steadiest coon dogs I have ever hunted with. She didn't have Rover's speed but when the old girl sat down and located the coon, she rarely missed getting the meat. That old ringtail would always be lying somewhere looking down at us.

I knew the Walkers would have their hands or paws full tonight. Pa had put his A team into this hunt. He knew these boys came to Egypt to beat his dogs and have the bragging rights to it. First, they had to get the job done and that was a tall order. You ever seen frog legs jump around in a skillet while being cooked, well I'll tell you that was the way mine were doing. Man I was so excited, my little old legs were shaking like leaves in the wind. I was rearing to get gone. This was gonna be a hunt to talk about around the winter fires for a mighty long time to come.

RC looked over at me disgusted, to him this was just another coon hunt, nothing more. Shoot he didn't even get excited over the Lone Ranger on radio while we were milking and to my way of thinking that was un-American. I got so excited once while I was milking old Beauty our Jersey milk cow, when Tonto, the Lone Ranger's sidekick, was fighting this jasper. I up and punched that old cow in the side and she dang near kicked me plumb to the fence. Yes sir, anyone not liking the Lone Ranger had to be some kind of foreigner or just plain crazy. We had a radio run by battery and sometimes Pa would sit it in the kitchen window and turn it on while we were doing our chores and milking.

As we stood there down at the rock crossing on Blue, my ears took in all the night critters along the River. The dogs were turned loose and we waited expectantly for the first long bawl of one of the hounds striking a hot track. I knew from experience if it was Rover all we would hear would be yip yip and that was only after he had that track red hot and Mister Coon on the run for home.

The river flowed smoothly along its sandy banks making hardly a sound as it drifted slowly past. Our carbides gave out eerie configurations as their light flickered out across the water. We all stood silently along the banks, no one breaking the stillness of the night, everyone listening expectantly.

Only minutes passed when one of the Walkers opened up with the prettiest and maybe the loudest bawl mouth my young ears had ever heard. Seconds later, I heard the unmistakable sound of Quane's lighter mouth strike then the other Walker fall in with them and the race was on. I'm telling you, those dogs took off downriver like they'd had turpentine poured on them. Man, the way they were moving, they had to have hit that track a second after that old ringtail laid it. I had to admit and so did RC for once, them Walkers were fast on a hot track. Quane was trailing last and we hadn't heard nary a thing out of Rover but that wasn't anything new. He ran a silent trail and seldom opened until he was almost on top of the coon.

The race slowed and then we heard one of the Walkers tap a tree. The second Walker stopped and went to treeing almost shaking the leaves out of that old pecan tree. I swear that hound was waking up that whole bottom. The two young men laughed and slapped each other on the back. Only problem was Quane didn't even slow down where the Walkers were treed. She just checked the tree they were on, then passed them two Walkers and traveled on another couple hundred yards before she gave out her locate bark, sat herself down and went to treeing.

Pa never said a word as the men laughed and cheered their hounds, but he knew. Quane had the coon up her tree. If the Walkers had a coon, she would have pulled up and treed with them. That coon had just tapped that tree and skedaddled on to a larger one.

"You boys go see what your dogs have and I'll go where mine is." Pa turned and started off with RC, a smirk splashed across his face, trailing along behind him. The young hunter who had offered me the pup looked kinda curiously at me as I walked away, but I knew. Those two Walkers were definitely barking up a bare tree. Quane seldom made a mistake when she treed. I could feel she hadn't made a mistake this time either.

Our two coon hunters just got started towards their dogs when the Walkers vacated their tree and ran to where Quane and Rover were treeing. Yep, Rover treed first I figured but with all the noise the Walkers were making no one heard him. Well that was the end of the laughing from our guests, nope not another peep came from either man as they followed us on to where the dogs were all looking up a huge, slick trunk pecan tree, just a bawling their heads off.

Sure enough halfway up the pecan sat Mister Coon snuggled up to a limb like a cockle burr to a cow's tail. Pa squalled a couple times and that old ringtail turned those eyes of his down on the commotion going on under him. You could tell by his unconcerned look that he weren't too worried. That pecan tree was bare of limbs, slick as a greased pig, and mighty big around. Old Mister Coon thought he was safe up there as if he were in a hollow. I don't figure he reckoned with the twenty-two rifle Pa was carrying or the climbing ability of RC Dennis.

Without a word, RC kicked out of his work boots and stepped up to that tree. The two men looked over at him, then up to where the coon was waiting. It was at least twenty feet to the first limb and after that, there still wasn't an abundance of limbs growing out of that old tree trunk.

"You gonna climb that slick tree?"

"Thought I'd give it a whirl." I knew RC was wondering what they thought he was gonna do when he kicked off his shoes, kick that tree over? But to his credit, he never uttered a word.

I'll say one thing for sure; RC could climb most any tree in these bottoms. He was probably the best tree climber in the county with the possible exception of Tim Dunn who must have been half monkey or something. When RC stuck his toes in that bark and started up, those four dogs went into a barking frenzy. They were sure 'nuff making a racket, the higher RC climbed the louder and faster they barked. You know, I was kinda proud of my uncle as he went up that tree. Them city boys couldn't believe it, all they could do was shake their heads in disbelief.

Pa slipped some lead ropes out of his pocket and caught Rover and Quane. "You boys catch your dogs and we'll let that old coon get a little head start on the dogs before we turn them loose after him."

"Do you think we can tree him again?" One of the men was doubtful. "We had'em jump out on us before and have never been able to tree them the second time."

"Well we'll sure give him a good run if we don't." Pa led Rover and Quane back away from the tree and looked straight up, watching as RC slowly made his way to where the coon was becoming a little nervous. Well maybe a little more than nervous, that coon was growling and hissing, slowly retreating out on the limb. I had to admire my uncle the way he could climb. I don't think the coon felt the same way though, he baled out as RC reached the limb he was on. Now some people would have thought it was a little unsportsmanlike of the coon to abandon the tree branch, but not RC, it saved him having to shimmy out on that little old limb and force the animal's evacuation.

To say the least Mister Coon made it to the ground a lot quicker than RC did. It always amazes me how a coon could free fall thirty feet, then get up and run off like they do. I've hunted many a year, well a few years and I've never yet seen one break a leg, not to mention their necks, taking the quick way down a tree headfirst. Coons were tough, probably as tough as any little animal I ever run up against.

Those Walker dogs were lunging and almost pulled our new friend's arms out of their sockets. Rover and Quane just stood there watching all the commotion in anticipation of the big race, their eyes darting from the frantic Walkers to the fast retreating coon. They weren't about to waste their energy jumping around all over the place. On that score, I have to admit they were smarter than the Walkers. Course now they'd probably been at it a little longer. Pa just stood there smiling slightly as RC climbed back down to the ground and put his shoes on.

That old coon had hit the ground running like his tail was on fire, man he sure lit a shuck out of there disappearing from site as RC finally got himself back into his shoes.

"Turn'em loose, boys." Pa waited and let the Walkers have a little head start. I had to admit he was a sportsman, letting them dogs have the jump like he did or had he already seen, like I did, the Walkers were a mite tuckered from the first race. Letting them lead the race would just tire them all the faster. Young hounds always want to be in the lead while they were on a hot trail.

What a race it turned out to be, what a race. I never heard such pretty music as them dogs was giving out. Nowadays city people would have been hollering for us to shut them dang dogs up, but that night it was beautiful. Like the country feller who was listening to the hounds bawling said to the city dude, "Man, ain't that pretty music?"

The city feller listened for a minute his ears all cocked then shook his head. "I can't hear anything for them dat burn dogs barking."

Yep, the race was on, RC took the lead, his long legs covering ground like a greyhound after a jackrabbit. I swear I hated it when he took off like that, my shorter legs just couldn't stay up, but I wasn't about to complain. Wouldn't have done me any good, he wouldn't wait on me anyhow. No sir, when you were out hunting with that boy, he had only one motto and that was mighty short and sweet, "every man for himself" and he meant it. I've been out late and got myself sleepy wanting to head for home. He'd just frown and tell me, pull up a piece of ground and go to sleep. A couple hours later, he'd come back and kick me to my feet. Why, I could have been ate by a hog or pounced on by Jackson's ornery bull, shucks maybe even snake bit. Didn't matter nary a bit, no sir, he was hunting and you didn't interrupt his hunting.

Back to the race, that old coon wasn't thinking tree this time, no sir he was in high gear and had run racing through his mind. Rover was in the lead, I could hear him yip now and then, but I figured the men thought their Walkers were leading the pack. Man, it was hot; the bottoms were steaming down along the river. Now I'm just a little skinny runt but I bet I done melted off twenty pounds in them bottoms. The coon was headed north and it looked like to me he had his sights set on the next county. Now a coon loping along looks like he ain't moving none too fast, but I can testify, them little fellers can up and tote the mail when they're a mind to.

The coon turned back east and at this rate, I figure we'd wind up almost in Coleman if something didn't happen soon. We lost Pa somewhere along the way which wasn't nothing new. We were young and could run. You know even though we stayed as close to the coon as we possibly could, Pa would nearly always be there with us when the dogs treed.

Again, the coon changed direction, doubling back south towards his own stomping grounds I reckon. Anyway we had run the little feller another five minutes or so when one of the Walkers came in to us. The other one lasted a little longer then he too was following us. Man was I ever disappointed and RC giving me that I told you so lopsided grin of his didn't help any. As they say, my bubble had been busted.

Up ahead, I heard Rover give his tree bark and sat down with Quane right behind him. Sure enough as we approached the small oak tree there Mister Ringtail sat, his eyes focused on us, shining like bright stars right into our lights. Our two city friends for once were silent as a dead rooster. Pa came walking up out of the dark trying to keep a straight face as he looked over to where the two Walkers lay panting in the grass.

"That was a race for sure." Pa looked up at the coon, for a big man he wasn't even breathing hard. One of these nights, I figured to stay with him and learn his secret instead of following RC all over the place like a chicken with his head cut off. "I'll guarantee you boys, that old gentleman up there has been run many a time in his life."

The men nodded as one spoke up. "Yes Sir, I expect he has."

"You boys want to run him again?" Pa was rubbing it in, pure innocently of course. He sure liked to have his fun at someone else's expense.

"I never heard of anyone treeing a coon two times in a night much less three times." One of the men stated.

Pa looked over at him. "Boys, I'll tell you what, let me water my dogs and I'll tree him all night long."

"Well Sir, I believe you, but if it's all the same to you we've had enough, and so have our dogs." One of the men looked down at the Walkers lying collapsed on the ground. "We still got to walk to the jeep, how far you reckon it is?"

RC looked over at me and rolled his eyes. Shucks these were young men. "Not far, maybe three, four miles." Course he was lying, it weren't over half a mile to the house but RC liked to have his fun listening to the men groan.

"You want to fight him?" Pa looked up at the coon.

The two men looked at each other and shook their heads. It made me feel bad, those boys sure had the look of beaten men and them Walkers definitely weren't as pretty as they were when this hunt started. They probably lost more weight than I had and their pretty coats were scratched and bloody from the thorns and briars, not to mention the mud all over them. Yes sir, they were a sore sight to look at. It was a plain fact of life, Blue Bottom had more than its fair share of briar patches, and a smart coon will run through every one he comes to.

I did learn one valuable lesson that night for a fact. Fat don't slip through briars near as easy as skinny does, on man or beast. However, fat does look better than skinny on most critters.

At Pa's last remark, I heard one of the men kinda croak out. "No Sir, just point us toward home. We couldn't fight that thing if we wanted to."

"You boys have good dogs; they're just too fat and out of shape for these hot bottoms." Pa looked over at the sweating men.

"So are we, I'm afraid." One of the men shook his head.

"You boys get'em in shape and come on back, we'll do it again."

"Mister Dennis, with all due respects, our dogs couldn't run with yours at any weight." The man grinned and patted Rover on the head.

Pa put Rover on a lead. "He's a coon dog, the best and so is she."

Well, we left the coon grinning and panting up that little old oak tree. I could have rung his ring-tailed neck because while he was helping Rover and Quane make them Walkers look bad, he was also knocking me out of getting my Walker pup. To this day, I've never seen them men again or my promised pup. Well anyway, that's the way that hunt went with the boys from Oklahoma City. I sure wish I knew their addresses because I might have dropped them a letter about the Walker pup that I never got.

Chapter 4
The Squirrels

Old man winter was slowly slipping away and the days were starting to get longer. I was sad in a way, but the outdoors was a calling now and I sure ain't talking about the garden or the fields. Young as I was, I knew we had to have garden vegetables to eat and the field crops for our stock. That caused one little problem and it was called work. A word, that at the time I wasn't too much in love with. Don't reckon I know why I worried so much about it though as poor old RC had to do most of the hard stuff while me and Joann watched from a nearby shade tree. I was always there to give him moral support, not that he wanted it. Now I ain't saying I didn't work, I did, but I also worked at getting out of work, which probably cost me more in the long run.

Yep, the days were starting to get warmer and Pa had RC in the fields plowing or harrowing, getting ready to plant. The fields had been broken and laid by for the winter but come spring they had to be loosened up a little. Now I was too little to hold up a walking plow but I wasn't too little to run that one row corn planter that I found myself a straddle of. Old Nail, the horse we used in single harness would plod along, trying to shake my liver loose. I would almost fall asleep until RC knocked me in the head with a fist size clod of Blue Bottom black land dirt. Seemed like I planted several rows of corn without realizing the planter was empty. I think the old mare thought I was loco, as we had to cover the same ground again.

Soon as we finished one field, next thing you knew we'd all be in the garden hoeing out the straight little rows that would soon start sprouting forth buds and vines. They were loaded with beans, tomatoes, squash, and everything else known to man. Now Pa had himself a garden that most folks today would call a ranch. I swear them rows got longer every time I looked down them.

Most people would work their middles with hoes. Nope not Pa, that garden was so big he'd hook Roadie our best garden mule to a Georgia Stock or Double Shovel and plow out the centers while we hoed around the plants. Now Roadie had her days, she could be as contrary as a mule, well she was a mule, but in the garden, she was a caution, that's where she shined. I never knew her to step on a single plant or give any problems. It was a garden loaded with vegetables and rabbits. I swear that garden drew rabbits like an old hound draws fleas. We ate the rabbits alright, we had them things fried, roasted, baked, in dumplings, no sir, Pa wasn't about to let them varmints eat his prize vegetables.

That makes me recall and I believe it was the same spring, just a little later after the garden was up and producing. We were all ready for school and Pa got the idea he wanted some snap beans gathered up before we left. Now I don't mean beans, I mean beans, a whole five gallon bucket full. You ever went to the garden for beans with a five-gallon bucket?

RC wanted to get to school to play basketball before classes took up, Joann wanted to get to school to talk with her flaky friends, and I just wanted to get. Like I said before, work just wasn't my long suit.

Yep, it was summer, school had taken back up by then, and the old garden was blossoming. Anyway, RC and Joann had connived on their way to the garden and come up with a plan. I figured it was Joann though; she actually was the brains of the outfit. I had to hand it to her, she didn't work much but she had a brain that could sure figure how to get us out of things. Course now, our backsides sometimes suffered on account of her thinking like she did.

The scheme sounded good to me all except the strapping I knew we were in store for when we got ourselves home. Course now, Joann would always play innocent, her being the pet of the family and Pa and Granny's youngest. She wasn't gonna get no strapping and she knew it so she was all for the plan. Me, even dumb as I was, I wasn't so sure. Well to make a long story real short, we up and filled that can with mush melons before we topped it off with beans. I had to admit we got to go to school earlier but all I did that day was look out the window and think about how mad Pa was gonna be when he ran out of beans and hit mush melons. You ever try to snap a mush melon, it's kinda messy.

I never could figure out why Pa didn't catch on to what we had done as we lit out of there like our britches were on fire. Granny on the other hand looked down at that bucket of beans and then back up at each one of us, but to her credit, she never said a word. I reckon she figured it was our hides that was gonna pay and it definitely turned out that way. I couldn't sit still all day for wondering how much of my bottom I was fixing to lose. I would have blamed it on RC and Joann for making me do it, but that was no good, cause then I'd had RC to face. Take my word for it his fists were a whole lot rougher than Pa's little old razor strap.

Well anyway enough of the beans, it's squirrel time. All that spring RC and me had been gathering enough boards and wire to build a sure enough, foolproof, bona fide, squirrel pen. Now you know a squirrel pen has to be tight or the little varmints will squeeze out. Pa would walk by from time to time and study on what we were up to. You might say he didn't trust us a whole lot, not that we were bad but for some reason we sure caused our fair share of mischief.

The big day finally came, we had the fields planted and ready, the wood boxes were full of kindling and firewood, matter of fact all our chores were done, we were itching to go. Calling to Rover, RC grabbed his single shot twenty-two and we headed for Alphie Rowland's bottoms, which lay right in behind the Egypt School House.

Rover treed several times and had the squirrels, but RC would call him off and we'd head on. Now old Rover sure didn't like it at all, it was the same as calling him a liar. He'd done figured RC had lost his mind as we walked off leaving them prime fat squirrels sitting untouched atop them trees. Well, the next time Rover treed solid we were deep in Alphie's briar and thorn patch and there was lots of it.

I figured us to be about a mile and a half from the house as the crow flies when the three of us gathered around the base of a dead tree. It had been hit by lightning and broke off at the top. Like I said that place was a maze, nothing grazed it but the small critters in it were plentiful. Shucks nothing of any size could squeeze in through the mess. Now old Alphie loved it though, I've heard him brag on that briar patch many times down at Murk's Store. Why I don't know, but Mister Rowland was kinda funny in ways. He had the right, as they said back then, he was the he hog of the county, meaning he had the money, shucks he even had a telephone.

We were standing there and Rover was treeing with every breath when RC seen a little ear peek out of that hole. Leastways he said later he did. What we were looking for was baby squirrels and RC didn't intend to go home empty-handed. Handing me the rifle he started shimmying up that old tree. Now for him it wasn't a hard tree to climb, and take my word for it coming down that morning was even easier. You wouldn't have believed in your wildest dreams what happened next. He was perched comfortable on the last limb and peered down in that black hole while me and Rover looked up expectantly. "Can't see nothing down there, it's pitch-black."

I would never have believed it if I hadn't of seen it with my own two eyes. RC reached down in his pocket and came out with a kitchen match. Back in those days, matches were made for striking; those things would strike on anything. Well he struck the match on the bottom of his pants and letting the sulphur take a good hold he let her go, yes sir, dropped that lit match smack-dab down that hole in the tree.

Whooee, it sounded like the Fourth of July going off right then and there. I don't know how far RC was blown from that limb; let's just say he didn't have any trouble reaching the ground. My eyes were blinking like a frogs in a hailstorm as I watched him hit and bounce about ten feet. Fire was shooting twenty feet out of the top of that dang hole as RC pulled himself together and grabbed the gun from me, hollering run! There sure wasn't any way of putting that fire out, no sir. You might say this time we had done it; the fat was in the fire. Come to think of it, he didn't need to tell me to run; I think my feet were running before I told them to.

Well you couldn't run through that jungle of woods but we weren't exactly doing bad. You might say fear kept me right on RC's heels. Rover had disappeared, the coward abandoned us both. He knew whatever came out of that hole he didn't want any part of it. We ran as fast as we could about a half mile before breaking into the open where we stopped to catch our breath and that's where Rover came to us. RC now, he was one that didn't get excited about much but I could tell he was relieved at seeing old Rover. He rather have lost me than have to explain to Pa how his best dog got burned up squirrel hunting. That would have been a curiosity alright. I'd of sure liked to have seen RC talk his way out of that one, but on the other hand, I sure didn't want for Old Rover to get burned up just to see the show.

Well our squirrel hunting was over for the day as we hightailed it for home. It was gonna be interesting to see how RC wiggled his way out of this mess. I swear every time I looked back the hair on my head stood up. Black smoke and flames were shooting thirty feet in the air and the wind was blowing right at us. That day my legs had no trouble keeping up, stark terror done it to me I'm sure. I'll bet I could have outrun Seabiscuit the racehorse that morning, for a fact.

Like I said it was Saturday, Pa and Granny along with Joann headed for Milburn at daylight to sell Granny's eggs and butter. The old farmhouse was vacant and lonesome looking when we hit that barbwire fence that separated our farm from John Lowes. RC put up his twenty-two, changed clothes, and then hit a high lope for the corral where his black mare was lotted.

Now I don't want to seem too critical about him leaving me all alone to face the music but that's exactly what he did alright. He bridled that mare and flung his skinny little rear across her withers before looking down at me.

"Don't say a word, if anybody asks I went to Fillmore early this morning."

That was all and well for him, but as I looked towards them flames a heading straight for the farm, I was wondering. First Rover and now RC was about to abandoned poor little old me that day, cowards the both of them.

"You think that fires gonna reach here?"

RC looked across the pasture. "No, there's nothing to feed it, it'll burn out soon as it runs out of timber."

Wrong, as I stood there and watched him and that little black mare head for the river in high gear, I kinda felt like a hog that was a fixing to get boiled. Me and Rover took us a seat on the front porch and watched the smoke and flames inching their way closer and closer to the farmhouse. Uh huh, nothing to feed it, looked to me like it was eating pretty good from where I sat, eating itself right towards the house.

I reckon my eyes were as big as saucers. I had guilt written all over me when George Dunn, his brother Jess, and his sons came rolling up in his old truck. "Where's Carl?"

"Gone to town, early this morning." Man was I glad to see them boys. Now I knew what the Princess felt like when the white knight in shining armor came to her rescue.

"RC?"

"Gone to Filmore." I lied convincingly then added lamely. "Early this morning."

They unloaded what firefighting equipment they had, which didn't amount to much back then, and stepped across the fence when several other men arrived from across the pasture. It was nip and tuck for a while that afternoon but a little before dark the fire finally gave up the ghost and slowly died out less than ten feet from our boundary fence. Well, me and Rover sat ourselves on that front porch and watched the whole show, and believe you me it was a dandy. Better than the Fourth of July when we accidentally set the fields on fire. Pa had brought his wore out team into the stomp yard earlier at a good clip and pitching me the lines he stared unbelievingly at the wall of smoke.

"Unharness the team and when they're cooled out good, turn'em loose." He didn't even slow down long enough to change out of his good town clothes which actually only consisted of a newer pair of overalls and a khaki shirt. He did exchange his good felt hat for the older work hat he wore.

Well just about like I figured, long about milking time RC showed up all out of breath, shocked at seeing all the men who had returned from fighting the fire standing around in the yard. They say a cat has nine lives and RC was going through his fast. I know for a fact when that tree exploded it scared me and Rover out of at least three of ours. I wasn't sure a dog had as many lives as a cat, probably not. Thinking back about it I still shake my head, RC should have been one of them movie actors, he put on quite a convincing show about being shocked at seeing the fire. The next day, which was Sunday, we found our baby squirrels or I should say Rover and Quane did. The kitchen matches stayed in RC's pocket where they should have stayed Saturday. To make matters worse, they were the worst pets I ever had. I'll tell you when those squirrels were little they were cute as all get out, but the older they got, the meaner they became. You best not reach in that pen or you'd come out with a nub for a finger. I only had ten fingers to start with and by the time nine of them were bleeding from bite marks, I lost interest in them squirrels completely. They finally up and disappeared. I never asked RC, but if I were a betting man, I'd lay odds they wound up as squirrel and dumplings. Didn't bother me none no sir, not one bit, as much as them things chewed on me, it was only fair for me to chew on them a bit. Folks that's how Rover got us the squirrels.

RC warned me not to say a word about the big fire, which for once I didn't. Seems the Wolf boys were blamed for it, someone had seen them playing with matches out in the woods. Twenty years later RC up and told the whole story to Pa, I reckon his conscience got the better of him. Nah, that ain't what happened at all, the boy didn't have a conscience but at least that's one strapping we missed and for once, I kept my mouth shut.

Chapter 5
Fence Posts

Once again, old man winter was upon us as the sun became shorter and shorter between morning and night. That meant the crops were in and the fields were laid by for next spring. Of course that didn't mean we could twiddle our fingers idly, no sir. Pa, he had other ideas. There was wood to get in, cows to milk, hogs to slop, and lo and behold up drives George Dunn, our nearest neighbor.

Now most times George was a welcome sight cause he always had a mighty good hound story or two to spin. George was a wolf hunter; he kept a pack of hounds that were mean enough to eat a full-grown grizzly bear for breakfast. You sure didn't want to get caught out in the woods with a cur dog of any type and have them hounds of his come roaring by. Many times, they've put me up a tree until they passed. Yes sir, I was deathly afraid them things would have me for supper.

Like I said, George Dunn was a storyteller, he could always sit back and spin a yarn keeping you fascinated until the last bark. Not this time, it weren't story-telling time. This visit was strictly business, seems George had a job he needed doing and you guessed it, RC was the prime subject. He needed about two hundred bois d'arc fence posts cut and split. The good thing was, he paid in cold hard cash that is, if there was anything good about work.

Most people know what bois d'arc or yellow sage is, and if you don't, I'll tell you. It's hard, mean, yellow and contrary, but those posts will last fifty years. George Dunn had just shook hands with Pa confirming the deal. When Carl Dennis gave you his hand, well it was as good as gold. The man did not and would not break his word once given. Times have definitely changed and back then, kids merely existed to work, nothing like today. Pa himself was a hard worker himself and he definitely meant to keep us boys working. He always threw in something about idle hands and mischief.

You ever cut bois d'arc with a two-man crosscut saw or try to split the logs with a sledge and wedges? We didn't have them newfangled chain saws back then, even if we had, bois d'arc wood would have probably eaten the chains like a kid eats Christmas candy. No sir, it was hard muscle and brains. That's where I came in; I supplied the brains, as I sure didn't have any muscles unless my mouth counted.

It was my job back then to pour river water over that crosscut saw to keep the blade cool and not ruin it. I've heard Pa say that bois d'arc is harder than a Republican Banker's heart. Being young, I had no dealings with any bankers but if their hearts were like that bois d'arc, they were some hard-hearted rascals, for sure. One thing it was sure good for though was making a longbow. Our good friend and neighbor Wilson Shico could sure make a bow. He was genuine, pure blood Choctaw Indian; always had a smile on his face and you knew you were always welcome in his house. His wife Pearl had the smallest kitchen. She cooked on a wood cookstove and her little kitchen was always blazing hot but her food was delicious. I can still hear her booming laugh as she hugged you or patted your back. Those two were the salt of the earth, the best of neighbors, and the best friends anyone could want.

Anyway, Pa wanted plenty of firewood in before we started on the log cutting adventure. He sent RC, my older uncle Keith who was in for a visit, and of course me and Rover down to the bottoms to resupply our woodpile. Back then, all we had for heat or cooking was wood stoves and they could eat up plenty of firewood over the winter. We hooked our work team Coaly and Lou to the wagon, pitched in the saws and axes, and off we went, I ain't saying merrily, but off we went.

It didn't matter that it was twenty degrees outside or that I was miserable to boot and complaining as usual. We had wood to cut and Pa meant for us to get after it. For some reason Pa thought the only good time to fetch wood in was on the coldest and nastiest of days and this one definitely fit the bill. You ever climbed into the back of a horse drawn wagon and bounced two miles down the road, freezing? If you ain't you should try it sometime, kinda makes you appreciate the finer things in life. I remember asking RC once in later years if he ever missed the good old days. After cutting his squinty eyes at me, his answer was short and sweet. "What good old days." Well he never was one to remember anything anyway, unless I owed him some marbles, then he never forgot.

At first things went pretty good, the wagon was about half-full of good seasoned limbs. We would take them home in one piece then cut them up on the old wood saddle. It was a lot faster than trying to cut the limbs in lengths out in the woods. Granny's wood cookstove needed smaller and shorter pieces of firewood and it was easier to cut them short at home. Them old axes were ringing and slicing into the oak limbs and I was busy toting and loading. Rover, who followed us, treed himself a squirrel off in the timber but when nobody came to the tree, he was disgusted and returned to where we were working.

Like I said, things were going tolerable well when wham, off came Keith's axe head and it landed blade first right between RC's eyes. Keith had hit a gusher for sure, blood was a spitting and spewing down all over RC's head as he tried to get his handkerchief from his pocket. I'll tell you, that blow would have killed a normal person but we all knew RC had an extra hard head. I knew that for a fact as one time he were a deviling me for no good reason as I was a sweet innocent child. Well anyway, I slipped up behind him and laid an oak axe handle over his head. I'm telling you he never even looked up, I swear to blue blazes, I don't think he even felt it.

Keith hollered over for me to hitch the team back to the wagon while he took axle grease from one of the wagon wheel hubs and gobbed it on the cut, then wrapped two large bandannas around RC's head. Doctors today would have fainted seeing all those germs being spread in the wound but between the grease and the freezing air, Keith got the blood stopped. Shucks, I figured any self-respecting germ would have froze to death quick, cold as that temperature was.

Keith clucked to the team and they hit a good clip back to the house thinking they would be fed and turned into the pasture. Keith went with RC inside leaving me and my frozen fingers to unharness and feed the team. Finished I slipped back into the nice warm house. That old wood stove was roaring red hot; boy it sure felt good as I backed my hind side up to it.

Granny had RC straddle a chair and was laying the alcohol to him. He was just sitting there quiet as a sulled possum, no sir, he wasn't about to holler but I knew he wanted to. I would have, ain't no pride in me when I'm hurting. Now in a fistfight, which I find myself in on a regular basis cause of my big mouth, I don't holler. If you do the feller whooping up on you is just gonna get surer of himself and hit you all the harder. Take my word for it, I know.

Wouldn't you know it, just when I'm getting toasty warm Granny finished wrapping RC up like a Christmas package and announces we can get back to work.

"Get back to work!" I protested quite loudly but to no avail. "RC ought to have stitches, be in a hospital, or at least in bed."

"Psssh." Granny scoffed. "He ain't hurt, nothing but a scratch, he's got a Dennis head."

"What if he goes back to bleeding or kicks the bucket on us or worse yet, starts hemorrhaging." Can't remember where I heard that terminology, reckon in school but it sounded good so I tossed it in for good measure. I sure didn't want to go back out into that cold air again.

Those sharp blue eyes of hers turned on me with a frown and I knew it was time for me to depart that nice warm spot by the fire. Before passing back through the door, I looked back. I swear, Toko, Granny's little dog who I had kicked away from the fire when I entered was back in his warm spot grinning at me. I swore vengeance on the little critter right then. He was deathly scared of someone with a sheet over their head running through the house. Uh huh, his time was coming.

We finished hauling firewood about milking time and RC hadn't bled to death or anything, so I still wasn't gonna get to warm up for a while. I have to admit he was tough, I would have been complaining with every ailment known to man. Folks back then didn't have us kids to look at, no siree bob, they seemed to have one purpose in life and that was for us young'uns to work.

My poor old fingers were so cold, old Beauty our Jersey cow tried to kick me as I eased them in between her leg and udder trying to get some feeling back into them. Those suckers had to have been frozen clear to my elbows. They didn't have child abuse back then, why I don't know. I reckon they missed their chance, cause right about then I was sure feeling abused.

We had our winter's wood in, not cut up but it was in the yard, a huge pile north of the house, all ready and waiting for the saw. We went on back to school for a week, then came Saturday morning. Bright and early right after breakfast, and milking, we were hip deep in bois d'arc logs working like beavers. It sure hadn't warmed up any but we already had several good trees down and RC and Pa were going at it with the old crosscut saw. Those two boys were in good shape, and that old saw was a singing a song as it ripped back and forth, yes sir rip rip, it was really purring. I kept up with them though, pouring water on that old saw every time it started to heat up. I even thought I broke a sweat once but it was just water flying off that wood.

Now Pa didn't hold with working on Sunday, so outside our usual chores of milking, slopping the hogs, and feeding the chickens we pretty much did whatever we wanted to. Every afternoon after school, we found ourselves back at them posts. I never admitted it but I was fairly put out with Mister Dunn for getting us in this predicament. Shoot, we could have used this time for squirrel or rabbit hunting, something worthwhile and fun. While we were working our fingers to the bone, I figured Mister Dunn was in the woods a hunting his dogs. Didn't seem quite fair to me but nobody listens to a kid. RC never said a word just

pointed at me and then towards the woods, like I said, he never was one
to waste time on words.

I had to admit though; those posts were piling up fast. RC was a
good worker. He didn't look it but he was strong as a horse and had
good staying power. With my supervision and encouragement, we were
definitely making headway on getting the job done. I always had an eye
out for them supervisor jobs.

You ought to have seen them posts all stacked up nice and neat
about halfway to the house along the bottom road, man they were a
pretty sight to behold. I figured it cost RC about fifty blisters putting
them there but we were finished and now we could hunt. Course now I
helped out all I could with the hauling and stacking those posts. Driving
that team back and forth, plus loading and unloading them heavy posts
was hard work. I had to admit the smell of fresh cut wood and the feeling
of accomplishing a hard job; well I reckon it was worth missing a few
hunts. That is as long as they didn't make a habit out of it, and Pa could
sure use the money they would bring.

Well sir, Mister Dunn had his posts, all two hundred of them
suckers, but he was a little slow in picking them up and moving them to
his home place south of us. Course now, they weren't hurting a thing
sitting where they were and there sure weren't any sense moving them
twice. He told Pa if'n it was alright with him he figured to get them
moved when he started building his new fence. Mister Dunn was kinda
like me, he didn't like to waste energy.

Early spring came and that's where the wreck happened, the heavy
early rains came with it. Blue River had a bad reputation about getting
out of its banks quicker than a hound could lick up a biscuit. It was a
nice little river but it could be treacherous as all get out when the rains
came from upriver. You go to bed and everything would be fine.
However, the next morning when you get up, there's old Blue only yards
from your potato patch up behind the milk lots, staring you smack-dab
in the eye with water everywhere.

Those two hundred fence posts were resting nice and peaceful right down along the road to the river crossing, trouble was that road was lowland and flood ground. Several times during the night, I heard Rover growl or whine. I was buried all nice and snug beneath several of Granny's heavy quilts, too tired or lazy to care, or pay much attention, so I didn't, apparently nobody else did either but we had to admit, he tried to warn us.

That morning Pa was up early as usual checking on his stock. All the horses, cows, everything was bunched up in the stomp lot which was unusual. It didn't take much figuring before he realized Blue was out of its banks and rising fast. The posts were an addition to the bottom so it didn't register in his mind that they were in dire straits or to put it plain, they were getting in deep water, about to be washed away down river, along with the two hundred dollars.

After breakfast, the milking finished, me and RC walked down to where we could see the river and I saw him stiffen. His eyes focused on the logs then the rising river and he quickly realized our hard work and Pa's money was in danger of being swept away. Mister Dunn hadn't taken delivery of his fence posts yet, so naturally we hadn't been paid. If those logs floated off down the river, it would be our loss. Hollering at the top of his lungs at Pa, we skedaddled fast as our legs would tote us back to the stomp lot to hitch up the teams.

"Hurry, tie the wagon beds down to the frames." RC barked orders as he led two teams over to the smokehouse where the harness was kept.

The teams were hitched and ready, everyone climbed in the wagons and started to the bottom where the posts already had two feet of water rising up around them. With Granny and Joann each driving, we started loading them two-dollar fence posts. Piling as many posts as we could into the wagons, we had to drive them to higher ground, unload, and return. This took precious time, the river was rising every minute and the horses were already wading in water almost to their bellies. Desperate, as the river was winning the race Pa finally looked to where I stood drenched to the bone, looking like a drowned rat. I'm telling you, I was beginning to downright despise those posts.

"Run to the Dunn's and get them back here in a hurry."

That's one thing I could do, I was young and I could run. Me and Rover took off like a shot. We passed the house and raced down the hill. Already the river was over the road that led to the county crossroads. The water was not over a foot deep but that was deep enough. I was just about to splash into that water when lo and behold right there in the middle of that water was a nasty looking fat little water moccasin. It had warmed up enough already and I reckoned as how the little monster was out early sunning himself.

Anyway, I looked like a good cow horse sliding to a stop right at the edge of that water. That old snake must have been washed out of his winter nest or maybe just an early bird, whatever it was he was right there and he was downright mad. Me and snakes didn't get along too good to start with so I wasn't about to challenge this one for the use of the road. I knew for a fact in the water he could swim faster than I could run. Trouble was I had to get to the Dunn's quick and this was the fastest way. Going back to the house and crossing the pasture would take longer, especially if I ran into Jackson's bull and had to hunt a tree. Yep, I had me a problem, a big problem for one so young. Grabbing a couple rocks I let fly thinking to run him off. Bad move on my part, that rock glanced off the snake's tough little body and the next thing I knew I had to run for my life. That thing was coming for me, but I wasn't waiting on him to arrive.

I started my retreat right then and there. You know a feller can get up a good head of steam quick with a mad water moccasin chasing him. I didn't look behind me for several feet and when I did Rover was a shaking that snake like a dishrag. I pulled to a stop and hurried back to where Mister Snake was getting the worst of the battle. Grabbing a good-sized stick, I was ready to wallop that moccasin good when his head parted company with his fat little body. Old Rover had chewed clean through that ugly tempered snake.

Patting the big dog's head, I took one look at that water and down the road I scampered. I was ashamed later as I never thought to check Rover for snake bite. With all his hair, I probably wouldn't have found any bite marks anyway. He seemed fine to me as we trotted on down the road towards the Dunns.

Luckily all of the Dunns were at home and in minutes we were racing back to help. We didn't save all of them posts but we got most of them out of the water. For years afterwards, every now and then while out hunting or fishing we'd find a post somewhere downriver and they always reminded us of our fencepost adventure. I would always think of Rover saving me from that water moccasin.

Rover was smart, intelligent beyond belief for a dog, and he had the heart of a lion, afraid of nothing. Yes sir, he was one of a kind, many a time he pulled my bacon out of the fire, never asking for anything in return. Mister Dunn paid for all two hundred posts as he felt losing a few of them was his fault. The new fence he built with those bois d'arc posts can still be seen standing today, the posts as stout as the day he took them home and built his new fence. Looking at that fence years later, I have to admire the hard work Pa and RC put into them split posts. I even wound up with a blister on my hand to prove I had actually worked. Course even with all my complaining that I was too injured to do my chores but I still had to get them done. Sometimes there just isn't any justice in this hard old world.

Chapter 6
John Lowe's Horses

It was Christmas time; snow was blanketing the countryside, something we didn't see much of. Outside it was serene and peaceful with quietness covering the woods and fields. It was a time of making snow ice cream, throwing snowballs at anyone who ventured outside, and sucking on huge icicles that hung from the eaves of the old farmhouse. It was cold; most of the wood animals were laid up warm and cozy inside their burrows or nests.

The cast iron wood stove in the front room was blazing red hot with a pan of raw peanuts roasting on top of it. Life didn't get any better. Our chores all done with nothing to do but laze around the house playing cards or dominoes and keeping warm and snug, yes sir, life was downright wonderful. It was Christmas Eve, almost time for the whole family to pile into the horse drawn wagon and head for Egypt School House, for our annual Christmas party.

The whole community would attend. No one would miss this grand event even in the worst of weather, there were just too many things to miss out on. I couldn't wait to get there. My friends would all be there, plus all kinds of cakes, candy, and music. I had to admit until I stuffed myself sick, the sweets were more important. Where candy and cake were concerned, it was indeed every man for himself.

Everyone but Pa was huddled underneath a canvas tarp and snuggled up in Granny's warm, thick quilts as the horses plodded the two miles to the schoolhouse. Snowflakes floated gently down on our heads as everyone sang Christmas Carols almost in time to the bells Granny tied on the horse's harness. We were happy, why wouldn't we be? Surrounded by family, no work to do, and fixing to have the time of our lives. As the man said, it was seventh heaven, it made your skin tingle with anticipation of the party.

Every kind of vehicle was parked or standing around what we used for a playground. Wagons and teams, trucks and cars were everywhere. Some of the younger crowd even rode their saddle horses. I didn't envy them for that because later when the party was over, it was gonna be a mighty chilly ride home. Riding a horse, beat walking, and they weren't about to miss the party. Ain't nothing like crawling astride a cold wet saddle and riding a few miles. Back then, folks were used to being cold, plus they were young and romantic. I watched the men as they stood around outside rolling their Bull Durham cigarettes, laughing and joking like it was summertime.

Spotting a familiar face, I pulled up short and started walking sideways towards the schoolhouse. Leon Perkins was there, standing next to the old merry-go-round, puffing on his habitual cigarette, and I sure wasn't taking my eyes off him. Leon was the one that flipped a cigarette butt down my pants when I was just a little feller. Hurt like the dickens and when I up and started jumping around like a bullfrog out of water, then let out with several bloodcurdling screams, I sure enough got my Mama's attention. You ever see an old cow protecting her calf, well that was Mama. Now old Leon denied it, saying it was merely an accident. I don't think my Mama believed him. Leon always had that lopsided grin on his face making him look guilty as an egg-sucking dog. There was no permanent damage 'cepting to my pants, they didn't fare so well. I gave him a scowl as we piled through the door, this time my Dad was with us and I weren't worried. Leon was wild but he wasn't stupid, and anybody that crossed A.C. Dennis had to be a little addled brained.

Inside we found the small schoolhouse brightly lit with coal oil lamps and decorated with Christmas spirit, and old Leon was quickly forgotten. Paper chains hung across the ceiling leading straight to the large cedar tree that was decorated with everything imaginable. Popcorn balls made with sorghum, dotted the big cedar tree along with peppermint canes and hard candy. Yep, this was gonna be a doozy of a party alright; I could already taste the food. I had plans on eating myself into a stupor and enjoying every minute of it.

Rumor had it that Santa Claus himself would be there. Well that would have been good too but I had already seen enough cake, pie, and candy to keep me occupied. Every person that went through them school doors got themselves a brown bag stuffed full of hard candy and fruit. Even Alphie Rowland got himself one, matter of fact his sack was twice as big as anyone else's. Course you have to remember, he was the he hog of the community, the one with all the money and land, for a fact he deserved the bigger sack.

Later we all had a good laugh on Mister Rowland, as his sack of candy turned out to be cold hard biscuits and cornbread. He laughed harder than anyone as he looked bewildered into his brown sack. It was all in good fun and later the brown sack was replaced with one full of candy. What a party it turned out to be, singing, eating, people talking and visiting, and chocked full of Christmas cheer. Even old Santa showed up that night but I had a strong suspicion he was too skinny. He looked and acted a whole lot like my Dad, A.C. Dennis. Course now, it might have been old Santa himself, maybe he was so thin because of the hard winter up north.

Dad disappeared right after arriving at the party and everyone thought he had left, but I still had my suspicions. He showed up again only minutes after Santa had given his final ho-ho-ho and disappeared out into the snowy night. Dad and Collie McGlaughlin got out their instruments and everyone had a great time singing the old time great Christmas songs. Collie McGlaughlin some called him Ed, was a whiz with a fiddle and Dad had his guitar and mandolin.

Now I always thought Santa went out through a chimney but the school didn't have one. Even this skinny Santa was too big to get up the stovepipe, besides at the time it was red hot. Anyway, it was quite a party and we all had an enjoyable time. Even the cold ride home in that bumpy wagon didn't dampen our night, snow was coming down lightly in the moonlight and it was just beautiful. Yes, those were the days, good fun, good food, and mostly good friends and family. I still thought that Santa was too skinny; they should have used Pa, now he looked like a full-blooded Santa Claus.

It was late February, it had been raining and Blue River was up. Not out of banks, but if you wanted to cross you better be half fish and able to swim. Breakfast was just completed; me and RC had finished with our chores and were fixing to go rabbit hunting when someone banged on the front door. Joann opened the door and stepped aside as John Lowe stooped a little to clear the door frame then made his way to where Pa was sitting beside the fire.

John Lowe was a tall, skinny man with the biggest Adam's apple I ever seen on a person and definitely the longest neck. When I first seen that thing bob up and down, I thought he had stuck something down his throat. He was a talker, now mind you, I hung out with RC and I wasn't used to much talking. If RC said ten words all day, I figured him to be sick. Anyhoo, old John went to talking and I could see right quick where this conversation was going and it wasn't good. RC who started getting that far away look in his eye like he wanted to be somewhere else sure wasn't liking it none neither, no sir, not one bit. Old Mister Lowe kept looking sideways at him, reminding me of a hungry man looking over the last piece of Sunday chicken.

The jest of the story it seems, was one of the Lowe girls was ailing and Mister Lowe wanted to get to Dodd's Drugstore in Milburn to fetch her some medicine. My money was on the liquor store, not that Milburn had one, but there was plenty of fellers around that kept quart jars stashed plumb full of homemade brew. I figured the man had run out of booze and needed a bottle bad. Not that he was a drunk but he did like a snort every now and then, mostly now. Problem was Pa let Mister

Lowe run his horses in with ours across the river where the grass was knee-high to a horse's belly. Yep, we had good bottomland pasture alright; and all of Mister Lowe's horses were in it, with several hundred feet of deep, fast water between us and them. John Lowe, lazy as he was, sure wasn't about to walk eight miles into town, and he positively sure wasn't about to swim Blue.

That reminds me, when Mister Lowe turned his critters in with ours a yellow stud colt over a year old was still running on his mama. Now I have to admit Pa questioned him about the yeller colt, as he sure didn't want his mares having any colts come spring. Horses weren't bringing a plug cent at the sale barn or soap factory, you couldn't give them away and Pa sure didn't want any colts out of this scrawny yearling for any price.

John Lowe slapped his leg and roared laughing. "Now Carl, you know he's too little and too young yet."

I reckon he was all them things but the funny thing was the following spring every mare we owned had a yellow colt at its side. Pa didn't find it too funny, well he should have known better than to take Mister Lowe's word on that little deal. Anyway back to our problem, John Lowe's horses were across the river and there was a lot of deep water between them and us. Pa hesitated, he didn't want to swim them across as Blue was up and running fast, and it would be a treacherous crossing. The more Pa said no, the more John Lowe argued and pleaded. Our whole livelihood depended on them horses. Without them, we sure wouldn't be doing any farm work. The bickering kept up for nigh on an hour and it didn't take long for me to figure out who was fixin' to win this argument.

Pa weren't no arguer and he was a man short on patience, especially when it came to Mister Lowe. Well just as I figured, Pa finally threw up his hands and gave up. I had to admit right then and there John Lowe was the best at arguing, yes sir he was a ring-tailed wizard when it came to flapping his tongue.

Looking over at RC, I could tell he was a wanting to strangle Mister Lowe and I didn't blame him one bit. That water was sure gonna be cold providing he didn't drown himself crossing. I kinda figure RC might have brought this on himself a little bit. John Lowe kinda had it in for him over the watermelon heist the previous summer and maybe this was his way of getting even. Whatever the reason, that river water was gonna be cold for sure.

Thinking back to those watermelons, I had to grin. Late last summer we were all sitting on the front porch. It was one fine evening, talking and enjoying the quiet of the night, when John Lowe ambled up to the porch with a couple of his kids in tow. Sitting down unasked he politely and straight to the point completely ruined a downright peaceful evening. Well RC was about to give up and sneak off when the talk turned to watermelons. Now let me tell you, RC prided himself on being a connoisseur of fine watermelons. In other more polite words, he would swipe a watermelon out from under a sitting hen without ruffling a feather. Now remember, he didn't do it just to be stealing, no sir, a man that could steal a watermelon and get away with it, well it just built your reputation in the community. Kinda like bank robbery, except they probably wouldn't toss you in the slammer for stealing a melon now and then. Anyway, John Lowe was a bragging and RC's ears were on point, just like a fine bird dog's tail.

Kinda like Bonnie and Clyde or John Dillinger who stole money, but of course RC only took watermelons and he sure didn't kill anybody. Couple of times I thought he was gonna beat me to death but I survived. Stealing watermelons was just a game and most of the time he returned them the next day. We didn't need any more of the things. Shucks we had a field full of them, take my word for it. I can vouch for that; I had to guard'em when they ripened to keep the coons and crows from ruining them. Them varmint's would peck a hole in the side of a ripe melon or punch one in with their paw, ruin it then move on to the next. I never figured which were the more contrary, a coon or a crow, I 'spect it was probably a tie. Now watermelons aren't a very enterprising business as everybody raised their own. They sure weren't gonna make a farmer rich but on a hot evening a nice cool melon sure made your taste buds smile.

Anyway, last summer John Lowe had himself a field full of prime melons. He was dead set on making sure none of the local boys beat him to them as they had in the past few years. Well sir, he ups and stacks every ripe watermelon he had on his front porch, then goes to Milburn or somewhere and buys him the biggest, ugliest bulldog he could find. Man, that dog invented ugly; the sucker didn't have any body, just teeth and claws. After Mister Lowe picked his melons and bought that animal, he shows up at the house bragging about how nobody was gonna make off with nary one of his hard-earned melons this year. He had that ferocious looking thing chained to his front porch to watch over his crop. That dog reminded me of an alligator crossed with a bobcat. It's a plumb wonder he didn't eat one of Mister Lowe's kids. He had thirteen, if he had lost one down the throat of that mangy gorilla, I doubt anyone would have missed the kid for quite a spell. I'll guarantee you that animal was all mouth and teeth, and he looked like he was serious minded enough to bite. I knew Mister Lowe had just thrown down the gauntlet; them were fighting words, or stealing words, whichever you want to call them. I knew RC was primed and ready, as he didn't care much for Mister Lowe anyway. There sure weren't no way he would ignore what was a downright dare. Now I got to admit I was a little nervous about going up to Mister Lowes after dark especially with larceny in mind. What if that thing was loose, why he could gobble up a little feller like me down in about two good bites. I just didn't relish them huge teeth of his sinking into my delicate hide. You didn't argue with RC when he has his mind made up, and like the man said, he was on a mission.

Another thing worried my poor little old brain, we still had to get by Mister Lowes other hounds. I remembered last summer sitting high on a load of hay that we were taking to G.O. Jacksons. Why from my bird's-eye perch, I counted thirteen kids and seventeen dogs in the yard as we passed and that ain't no exaggeration. On top of that, they weren't any of them mangy pot lickers of his sociable towards strangers. My doubts and grumbling didn't matter a smidgen, no sir. RC was going and he aimed for me to be right there with him, you know, an accomplice in crime. Shucks it was in my mind he might use me for bait if the side meat didn't keep that hound occupied. One thing was dead certain, he was gonna bring home them watermelons, one way or another.

Right about midnight, we raided Granny's kitchen. Then we checked down in the well and took every piece of side meat and leftovers we could find, loading one of Granny's lard buckets to the hilt. I looked forlornly back at the old house and safety as we hauled and pushed the two-wheel cart that we were fixing to use to haul off them melons, providing we didn't get ate. How did I ever let RC get me into these predicaments? I had to admit though, I was more scared of him saying I was chicken than I was of that bulldog. All he had to do was holler frog and I started to jumping, yes siree. You know I kinda enjoyed taking part, excepting of course for the last part where my backsides met up with Pa's razor strap. It turned out that old bulldog was a real pussycat or just plain hungry. Whichever it was, with a little persuasion from that lard bucket, he became meek as a lamb and the rest of them no-account hounds didn't even wake up. Neither did Mister Lowe, I could hear him caterwauling at the other end of the porch while we were carting off his melons. I mean the man had him a cot on the porch within eyeshot of his prize melons and he was snoring so loud he should have woke up the dead.

Come morning after a lot of hard work them melons and that bulldog were a sitting on or tied to our front porch. You should have seen the look on Mister Lowe's face when he came puffing to our house to report the theft and seen his dog and melons sitting there as quiet as could be.

RC was all puffed up like a preening tom turkey. He swore with a straight face, he knew absolutely nothing about the melons or how they managed to get themselves on our front porch. RC wasn't too much of the laughing kind but after Mister Lowe steamed off towards home I thought the boy was gonna bust himself a gut right there. Now he had bragging rights at school as having pulled off the best watermelon heist in the county. Course now I didn't figure that line of work would make him rich but it sure did give him prestige in school when the other boys found out about the escapade. That old gentle guard dog, why after RC got through telling about the battle he had pulling every melon outta that ferocious dog's growling face, the school kids were plain scared to go anywhere near the Lowe farm.

It made for a good laugh of course and Pa didn't even strap us for it. I think Mister Lowe never forgave RC for that little stunt so here we were in this fine pickle. Don't forget, we had to haul them danged melons back home. Mister Lowe was a little put out with his guard dog, said as how we could keep the dog but Pa put his foot down to that line of thinking real quick like.

Back to the horses, Pa was riled alright. "RC go across the river and catch Lou, put the bell on her, then bring them in a bunch down to the crossing."

"Yes Sir." Normally the herd would follow the bell mare kinda like the Judas goat of the Bible. I learned that from the Baptist Church in Milburn, and our preacher Mister Tom Caldwell.

"Whoa up there Carl." John Lowe just had to put his two cents in again. "Put that bell on Betty, she'll bring'em across. Why she's half water duck and half snapping turtle."

Our farm had an old train trestle still standing at the high bank of the river bend that use to anchor the railroad bridge crossing Blue. All that was left of it was the concrete bunkers on each side, but that was where RC liked to hit the water and swim across when the river was high. Logs, brush, all kinds of debris drifted with the current as we all stood there waiting while RC stripped down. A slight drizzle fell making me shiver in spite of myself, man it was cold. I just knew RC was fixin' to catch his death. This was crazy, but you still had to admire him, braving the cold then the dangerous swim, and then he still had to find the horses on the other side. Now running around in cutoff jeans, in freezing rain, in the middle of February looking for a bunch of horses ain't exactly my idea of having fun.

Rover stood there watching the proceedings with us. Pa didn't want to send Rover alone, someone needed to put the bell on one of the mares. The river was in flood and the current was mighty fast at the crossing, the horses needed to hit it and swim straight across. Downstream less than two hundred feet was a huge log jam. If the horses turned down that way, they'd get hung up there and probably drown. It would be almost impossible to get them to swim back upstream against the current to where they could get out. In the bend of the river where the log jam was lodged the riverbanks was steep and impossible to climb.

"Now boy, you kick old Betty in first, she'll bring'em across."

RC only looked coldly at Mister Lowe as he bailed off into that fast moving water. Rover was right beside him as they stroked hard for the other side. Splashing ashore RC never looked back as he disappeared into the woods with Rover following silently behind him. We all knew the dog would lead RC straight to the horses but he wanted to catch Betty and get the bell on her, before the herd started running for the crossing. Sure enough, less than ten minutes passed when the horses could be heard coming at a hard lope for the river.

RC was astraddle of Betty and he had the bell strapped around her neck. We could hear it banging as she loped along. I didn't figure the horses would attempt the crossing but like Mister Lowe said, Betty was a water duck. She hit the water a stroking for the far shore without even breaking stride. Rover was behind the herd, baying and pushing the younger horses from the back. It was quite a sight to watch fifty or more horses swimming across that swift current, their necks stretched to their fullest, their nostrils distended, only their heads, ears, and a little neck showing. Old Rover hit the water behind the last colt and it was a good thing he did.

Things were looking good as the horses reached midstream, that's when Betty the water duck turned mule headed. She took the studs and headed straight downstream, into the log jam. RC didn't have a bridle or anything to turn her and his fists up against her thick head was to no avail. All he could do was bail off her and grab onto Coaly as he and Lou swam by. Rover went straight at the horse's heads and started barking.

With RC's help through sheer determination and will power, they managed to turn most of the bunch towards the far bank and safety.

Seeing that the rest of the horses straightened out and were heading straight across, Rover swam to the rear and was nipping and crowding the horses in the rear. He kept them headed for the far side and shallow water. Most of the herd managed to swim out of the deep water and waded into the back water of the higher fields. Only the colts were still in danger as they swam beside their mothers who were now in water barely above their bellies. Mister Lowe's Betty along with my little mare Trixie, Nail, and at least twelve others were hung up in the calm water of the log jam. The horses seemed to be floating and just bobbing around in the deep water. I stood there staring at poor Trixie and cussing John Lowe and his water duck Betty, under my breath of course. Pa wouldn't stand for us young'uns to sass a grown up, no sir, not for any reason, right or wrong.

RC ran up beside us after he got the others headed for home. "Run to the house and get your Dad. Tell him to bring ropes and come on the run."

I made that short dash to the house in record time even for me. Less than a couple minutes later, I was racing behind Dad back to the river. Both RC and Dad were strong swimmers and they were both in good shape. Hitting the water and staying out of reach of the swimming horses, Dad would rope a horse and swimming back upstream. He would pull on the horse while RC and Rover pushed it from behind.

I never thought they'd save a single head but with a Herculean effort, not a horse perished in those floodwaters. After three or four horses were pulled out, the rest finally followed the next one upstream and they all were saved. Like I said, RC and Dad were great swimmers. They had to have been to swim that current upstream so many times, but they had help, Rover was there all the way doing what he could to save the day.

Mister Lowe never uttered a word as he caught his horses and left for home. It was probably for the best. Pa always treated his neighbors the very best, but Dad; well let's just say he was a breed apart. Little old me, sitting perched up there on the old railroad right-of-way making sure I didn't miss a thing, was wondering why my little mare Trixie was the last to come out of that river. When I asked why, RC was ready. He said, he'd been hollering for them to get her first but they ignored him. The answer I received later was they got the good horses out first and the dinks last. Kinda hurt my feelings at the time, but what the heck she was safe and sound, that's what mattered most. I knew who had the best horse of the bunch.

Well John Lowe got his horses but he lost his good graze on free grass. Nope, Pa wouldn't let him bring his horses back. Reckon though Mister Lowe had the last laugh as early spring had brought us the bumper crop of worthless yellow colts swimming at their mother's sides. They did add a little color to the place, weren't worth a plug nickel of anybody's money but they sure had plenty of yellow on them.

You know that little swim in the middle of winter should have broke RC from stealing peoples watermelons but it didn't. The boy was just plain hardheaded.

Chapter 7
G.O. Jackson's Bull

Saturday morning found the whole family settled nicely in the back of the wagon. Snip and Coaly had the privilege of pulling the wagon into the nearest town, which was Milburn. Every Saturday morning normally found one of the family hauling Granny's eggs and butter into town to swap at Murk's General Store for whatever we needed. This Saturday everyone with the exception of RC was going. That boy just didn't cotton to people nor town. Milburn was eight miles away, eight miles of gravel roads and that old wagon didn't come equipped with springs. Those old metal wheels would screech and crunch against the gravel road in places, making you want to cover your ears.

Me, I was young, the bumping and jarring didn't faze me in the least. I had me a long string and I'd pull my red truck along behind the wagon all the way into town. I'd be bouncing in and out of that wagon like a yoyo trying to keep the little truck upright on its wheels. Now that was a trick in itself, as every rock or rut tipped the truck over, more trouble than it probably was worth. It kept me occupied and out of trouble. I figured I was a mite old to be playing with trucks it covered up for my more sinister plans along the way.

When I wasn't being watched close, I had me another little game that kept me more than busy, helped pass the time and it was kinda enjoyable. Every farmhouse back then had a passel of hounds that always came running to bark and snarl, raising a ruckus around our wagon until we managed to escape on down the road. The noise was deafening and none of the owners were overly concerned with me going deaf or scaring our horses. Course now, Snip and Coaly were older workhorses so the dogs didn't faze them in the least. It sure 'nuff fazed me though, that confounded barking interrupted my truck pulling. A couple years earlier when one big old black and tan hound jumped atop my poor little old truck and broke the string, that did it, I was out for revenge. Poor Granny, she knew exactly why I pulled that truck too town, cause I sure didn't play with it at home. To her credit, she never said a word, just shook her head when a dog started squealing and hollering.

Pa was usually preoccupied with waving and smiling at the passing neighbors. Sometimes he would stop a minute and pass the time of day, which allowed me time enough to do what I had to do. Pretending I was setting my truck back on its wheels, I would slip an old tow sack over the side of that wagon and tie it to the rear wagon wheel. The minute the wagon resumed its journey to town that sack would go to flopping around and around and then it was kinda like fishing. Every now and then, you'd get a bite and then the unlucky hound that did the biting would get the ride of his life. It always amazed me that a dog could grab that sack but they sure couldn't turn it loose, at least not until they took a few good laps around that wheel. I've got to admit, I didn't figure out this little trick by myself, nope RC put me on to it. Part he didn't tell me until it was too late was what Pa would do to my backside when he caught me. It kinda upset the neighbors when they saw their favorite hound flopping around that wheel like he had conniption fits or something. Pa sure wouldn't stand for his friends and neighbors to be upset.

Course now, the hound would go to growling which would turn into whining, then after a few rolls on the ground would turn into some serious howling. Naturally all the commotion made everyone look back to see what was happening. 'Bout that time the dog would finally break himself loose and hightail it out of there, if not, I had my trusty slingshot to hurry him on his way. I've got to admit the shocked look on my face as I was trying to figure out what happened to that poor old dog didn't convince anyone. Most times, it kept me from getting a strapping.

"Reckon he got caught under a wheel, Pa." I said innocently shrugging my shoulders.

Like my old Daddy used to say, a catfish wouldn't get caught if he'd keep his mouth shut. It never hurt the hound any and I figured I was just helping out a bit with his education. Was kinda funny though, next time we passed that dog, he upped and looked the other way. Way I had it figured, I was doing him a good turn. In the end though, they were definitely sack broke if there was such a thing. Don't guess I ever caught the same critter twice but it sure weren't from lack of trying.

Well on to town we went, that old wagon just a bouncing and crunching gravel under its iron wheels. Kinda monotonous if you know what I mean but it sure beat walking. Saturday always found several families in town doing their shopping, plus a whole passel of farm kids. That's where things got kinda interesting. Milburn had a whole mess of city kids just waiting to show us farm kids the error of our ways.

We went to Egypt School House so we didn't know the town kids very well. Oh we knew them well enough I reckon, at least my nose did. They figured we were trespassing in their town and just had to start something. Pa always took the time to tell me to be good and not get in any trouble. You know, family respectability and all that, and Pa was highly respected in Milburn. I always put on my innocent face as I stood there looking up at him. Shucks a poor little innocent thing like me couldn't possibly start anything, no sir.

Somehow though, I always managed to get back home with a black eye or maybe a bloody nose. My smart mouth and my natural ability with a marble was the usual reason. Sometimes us farm boys were lucky and won a few marbles from the city kids and that was what would normally start the ruckus. Marbles were a valuable asset to a boy back then with everybody carrying a pocketful of them. Anyway, a good set was worth it, that is, if you won some marbles. A good scuffle as long as it was out of Pa's sight never hurt anything. Like I heard a feller tell his wife once, a good fight kinda took the steam and meanness out of a man. Course now, I weren't no man yet by a few years, but let me tell you, like that feller told his wife, a few knuckles against your eye and nose will definitely take some of the pepper out of you.

Other than a good fight, another thing enjoyable about our town trips was the ride home. Mister Murk always gave us kids a brown bag full of hard candy, which if ate slowly would last us a couple of weeks. We would suck on a couple pieces of that candy, then Granny would fill us up the rest of the way on bologna and mustard sandwiches and pickles. Yep, there me and Joann sat kicked back on some quilts, a sandwich in one hand and a Nehi Orange Soda Pop in the other, a boy couldn't ask for any better life. RC sure didn't know what he was missing. After I polished off my sandwich, Pa would always let me drive the rest of the way home if I pestered him enough. It sure made me feel like a man, standing in the front of the wagon, the lines in my hands, my chest all puffed out.

Now G.O. Jackson was our neighbor down the road and he was the county commissioner for our part of Johnston County. He ran cattle on land across Blue River and that meant his cattle and his Hereford Bull ran alongside ours with just a barbwire fence separating them and that's where the problem came in. Mister Jackson's bull liked the ladies and he sure didn't show much respect for that fence, going and coming whenever and wherever he had a mind to.

That little old bull wasn't much to look at, small in size, but he was quick as a cat. My first encounter with the sorry little sucker probably was the result of me placing a well-aimed rock at his backside with my slingshot. That thing was equipped with red rubber from inner tubes that would really stretch and could send a rock humming, fast, hard, and accurate. Nothing like the sorry black stuff we've got for inner tubes today, which won't stretch worth a durn. Now to my way of thinking, he should have made a hasty retreat back to his side of the fence. Nope it didn't happen that way at all, that little bull whirled around quicker than a good cow horse. After locating me here, he came on the run, faster than a chicken after a June bug.

Yep, he was in hot pursuit and I was in full retreat. I reached the safety of the first tree I came to and nimbly climbed into its low branches. Below me, blowing snot and staring up at me, was Mister Bull. Well, I still had my trusty slingshot and several rocks. I didn't figure the bull could climb, so I was armed and fearless from where I was perched.

I let it fly and dust flew from the bull's head, I had hit that sucker right smack-dab between his eyeballs. Surely, I figured this time he'd beat a hasty retreat out of there, but no, that little bull rammed his hard head into the oak almost dislodging me from my safe haven. Now things were beginning to get a little out of hand to say the least. I sure hoped that little old tree would hold up, for it wasn't looking near as safe or strong as it once did.

I wasn't about to smack him with another rock, nope I learned better than that. Screaming for help was a possibility but the house was way across the river completely out of earshot. Besides, I wasn't about to let anyone know of this mess I'd got myself into. I wasn't supposed to come this far from the house alone to start with. Caught over here across the river would get me a good strapping at the least. I figured in time the bull would surely lose interest in me and go about his business, that is, if I remained silent and didn't bash him with another rock.

Two hours later I was beginning to worry, that stupid animal was still standing around under that tree pawing the ground every once in awhile. There I sat, still perched on that limb like a hoot owl. Once, he had ambled back towards the fence, but I hardly dropped to the ground when the smart aleck spied me and came on the run. Scampering back up on that limb, I was about to lose my patience. I hadn't figured out what good that was gonna do me but I was getting mad.

It was late in the afternoon and milking time was coming on. I had to do something and quick, I was surprised my Mother didn't have half the county out looking for me already. Suddenly it dawned on me; Rover would be coming after the cows anytime now. Whistling as loud as I could, then hollering I waited several minutes then let go again. This went on for about thirty minutes when I spied my savior coming at a run across the field. Man was he ever a sight for sore eyes.

I knew relief was on the way, so I up and loaded my slingshot again and let fly. This time I beaned him one right on his left ear, yep dead center. Shaking his white face, he banged the tree again. Now I've had mama cows run me before and even our bull treed me once but this bull was a persistent cuss to say the least. I just couldn't figure what he was so riled about. Shucks, I bounced pebbles off of everything on the farm at least once. I remember once shooting at some tin cans and accidentally killed Granny's favorite rooster. At least that was the story. She wasn't too happy but there weren't no use in wasting him. Granny turned that poor old rooster into some good chicken and dumplings that we had on Sunday. Don't remember her eating any though. Anyway, seeing Rover coming to my rescue, I ricocheted another rock off the bull just as he arrived on the scene.

I figured the way that old bull blew up and charged Rover the two hadn't had any face to face dealings as of yet. Well that was fixing to change as I hissed the big red dog onto that little pile of meanness. It was quite a battle for a short period of time but a few bites to his tender nose and heels and Mister Bull made a quick exit back across the fence. With a swagger, I hissed Rover after the cows while I strolled cockily back towards the river strutting like a banty rooster, so proud of myself. Bad move, I should have watched behind me a lot closer.

I was almost to the water when I looked back and all I seen was that bundle of red orneriness as he tore across that field only a couple jumps behind me. Rover was nowhere in sight so I had to hit high gear out of there taking off as fast as my little old legs could run for the crossing. I'll tell you for a fact, I looked like a quarter horse leaving there, cause that bull had pure hate and discontent on his little brain and he had me dead in his sights. I didn't spy any trees small enough for me to climb quickly and I sure wasn't in the mood to sit up a tree again even if I had. Leastways now, I was back nearer the river crossing, closer to where I was supposed to be.

That bull was beginning to get on my nerves and I was already thinking of some kind of revenge as I sprinted towards the river. Old red was blowing snot up my backside when I bailed out into the deepest part of the creek. This time, I didn't have time to check for snakes, anyway I figured they were a lot less dangerous than the bull. I never hesitated once about hitting that water and stroking for the other side. Mister Bull pulled up right at the river's edge and pawed the ground. I can say one thing for him as he slid to the edge of the river; he sure had a quarter horse stop on him. He stood there pawing and snorting, but made no attempt to hit the deep water. I reckoned maybe, he couldn't swim. I'd have to remember that in case I ran into him again. He didn't forget, for a bona fide fact that little bull held a grudge. Less than a week later, he had me and RC in his sights and up a tree practically in the same spot. Now bullying a little feller like me was one thing but RC, uh-huh now that was a horse of another color. Course here we were, RC was in a tizzy almost ready to shoot the dang bull but Pa would probably have to pay for it and that definitely wouldn't be a good idea. RC just couldn't figure out why the little bull had suddenly become so mean and I dang sure wasn't about to tell him. He'd have probably thrown me down with the thing if I had. Course now, there was always blackmail, what if the kids in school found out RC let a little bull like that tree him?

"You want me to put a rock upside his head?" Well it was an idea, cause I knew what was fixing to happen the second that rock and that bull met up. Before RC could answer one way or the other, old Rover came to our rescue again. I'm sure glad that old dog couldn't talk. All the way home RC mumbled under his breath, I knew he would come up with something for Mister Bull. Seems that RC had torn his Levi's going up that tree and clothes were something we didn't have an abundance of. Now, what if I stretched that tear a little when I told the kids? Course now, that could result in me getting another good lickin', as RC wasn't anybody to fool with when he was a mite disturbed.

It was two weeks later, yes sir I recall the date vividly in my small brain, me and RC was heading home from a successful fishing trip down on Blue. It was almost milking time; Rover was pushing our cows towards the stomp lot passing less than fifty feet from where we stood behind a pecan tree watching. I recognized that mangy red coat of Mister Jackson's bull about the same time RC did. Today though, he weren't causing any trouble, he was just following along behind the herd of milk cows, quiet as a mouse.

It wasn't that we were afraid of that little bull, we were just being cautious and for safety sake. We followed along behind at a good safe distance. I done found out that little old red bull could run a lick, shucks I figured he was faster than a greyhound dog after a jackrabbit. I for one wasn't taking any chances of him catching me on open ground. Well, we all started up the lane leading to the stomp lot, cows, dog, boys, and one red bull. The fences were getting closer and we felt a little more comfortable so we closed in on the cows some. The road leading to the house and stomp lots climbed a little, then it leveled out letting you get a good view of the stomp lot and feed troughs.

We got ourselves a good view alright, our eyes were bugged out like a frogs on a lily pad, man what a show. Pa was crossing the flat lot whistling an old tune he always did when he was in a good mood and just casually looking towards the cows. I reckon he didn't see the bull or didn't pay him any mind. Whichever it were, it was one big mistake. That little bull spotted Pa swinging them buckets and he was in hot pursuit. Pa looked up and all he saw was a big set of horns and mad bull charging straight at him.

Now Pa was a big man himself but that old bull had nothing on him for quickness. Throwing those milk buckets straight into the air, Pa looked like a baseball player stealing third base as he slid under one of them long feed troughs. Course now that wasn't a real good idea as the bull followed right along behind him, yes sir, slid right in under that wood trough, all thousand pounds of him. Me and RC stood there bug eyed, frozen in place, our mouths catching flies, stunned and shocked to the bone to say the least.

Anyway, when the bull didn't all fit under the trough, he threw his head in high gear and knocked that trough off its legs and straight upwards. I just knew it was curtains for Pa this time, his legs were running but his body didn't seem to be moving. Luckily, the wooden trough came down on the bull's head giving him a temporary setback and giving Pa a second's reprieve and time to make his escape. I swear he should have been in those Olympics I heard about, because let me tell you from an eyewitness account, he cleared that pole fence in one leap. I'd seen that bull jump and he was good, maybe not in Pa's class but he could clear a five-strand fence, I'll vouch for that. I stood there my mouth opening and closing knowing the next jump would land the bull and Pa in the same lot together. If he did it was gonna get mighty interesting as that lot wasn't all that big, leastways not near big enough for the two of them.

Bout that time Rover entered the fray and that was that. After Pa caught his wind and the red bull left his face, he left RC to milk. Pa and Rover started the bull home to Mister Jackson's house. I sure would have liked to have been there and listened to the tongue-lashing that I knew Mister Jackson was fixing to get. I always liked Mister Jackson; don't think RC was overly fond of him. RC worked for Mister Jackson at his peanut warehouse in Tishomingo and there was some kinda of difference about some money. I figure RC got his money but nothing else was said of the matter. Anyway, I knew it sure would have been interesting to listen to the upcoming lecture I figured he was in for.

Apparently it didn't work out that way though, seems our neighbor somehow convinced Pa that it had to of been something me and RC done to that bull as he had always been gentle as a lamb. I'll tell you, one look at Pa's or RC clothes and you'd forget that idea. Gentle as a lamb, right, some lamb. Anyhoo, I guess you can say we got the blame again, although they couldn't prove anything on us. Like the man said, they didn't have the dead wood on us so we didn't get in trouble but you could tell by the slanty look of their eyes they were thinking it.

It was kinda funny though, for a long time after the bull incident Pa would always make sure he was in the safety of the milk lots when Rover brought the cattle in for milking. I figured Mister Jackson would keep his bull on his side of the road but that didn't happen either. Anyway, I made sure to steer clear of that critter or have my trusty bodyguard Rover with me when I crossed the river.

Yea, that little old bull stayed around for several years but for some reason he mellowed out. I reckon he just got tired of chasing me up a tree then waiting in vain for me to come down. Course as I grew I got faster on my feet, not in the bull's league but I could run. I wished I had a nickel for every rock I bounced off that little critter. Course I made sure I didn't make a mistake and climb a small tree anymore either.

Chapter 8
George Dunn's Hounds

Things were running pretty smooth around the old farm. The chickens were laying good, which while making Granny more money, it also made more work for me and Joann. It was our job to gather, wash, and candle them things before placing them in their cartons. Our shoats were fattening up fast and the cows were all milking heavy with mostly bull calves on their sides. It was coming on winter again, that meant school was in, the garden and field crops were harvested for the year and the ground laid by for next year. The corncrib was crammed plumb full, our hay was stacked, and thank goodness, the garden had coughed up its last vegetable or grass root, hallelujah. Now I don't consider myself a lazy person, I think RC might think I have a tendency to avoid work, but not me. Nope, you might say I believe in conserving my energy is all and I'm good at it. Now with winter coming on, I had plenty of time to conserve it even more.

All we had to do was our chores, school, bring in the firewood, and go hunting. Yippee, now that's the life. I was young and loved to hunt. That's about the only thing that I didn't mind expending energy on. Now all the entertainment we had besides cards and dominoes was coon or squirrel hunting, problem was, nobody wanted me for a partner in games so I usually had to watch. Pa and Granny would have had better luck playing against me and Toko, Granny's little dog rather than RC and Joann. Leastways I never stacked the cards, so they say in gambling when you cheat, and I didn't figure Toko knew how. Now, how do you think I felt sitting there leaning back against the wall of the house with Granny's lapdog, just a watching everybody else laugh and slap the table, having a great time?

The next day the weather turned cold and the clouds rolled in. It looked like it could turn into a bad winter so Pa ordered more kindling to be brought in and stacked. Reckon you figured out who the kindling man was. Yep, it was me. RC split wood and it was my job to get the kindling and to fill the wood boxes.

That kindling always reminds me of years back when I was a lot younger. Joann and me use to keep a lot of stick horses tied to the fence out north of the house. RC told us that Pa had at least fifty horses at all times, in case some crippled so we should keep just as many. Well almost every morning, we'd wake to find some of our horses gone. Now we thought we had them tied good and snug with the binder twine we used for bridles. We just couldn't figure out how they were getting loose. RC would just stand there and shake his head in disbelief as we told our story. Shucks, I'd even have Rover stand guard over them at night. You guessed it, them suckers still got loose somehow.

Anyway, back to the bottom we'd go to cut us some more horses. This went on for some time and I sure wanted to catch me a horse thief bad. Well, we definitely should have been watching for horse thieves alright, only closer to home. I told Joann them exact words but we followed RC's advice and kept bringing in more and more horses and lining them up and down that old fence. One thing we hadn't figured out was that at that time RC was the one responsible for keeping plenty of kindling on hand for Granny. Now he was a hard worker, of that I had no doubt. However, if he could figure out a way for you to do part of the work, it sure didn't bother his conscience in the least.

One day, I found this real straight hickory limb. I carved and whittled on that little old limb to make it look just like a paint horse. I was really proud of the new addition to my herd that night as I rode him back and forth in front of the house. I made sure to tie old paint doubly good to keep him from wandering away during the night.

The next morning I walked outside at first light, lo and behold old paint was gone. RC just shook his head in amazement and blamed it on the Wolf boys, just as later on we would blame them for the big fire. No account injuns, stealing my good saddle horses. Well I was down in the dumps for sure. I had half a mind to walk over to their place and dish out a few black eyes. Only problem with that was, there were more of them than there was of me and they were a lot bigger. I would probably be the one winding up with black eyes. Now black eyes didn't bother me all that much, that is if I could get in a couple licks of my own. Shucks, I was always toting one around but I wasn't completely convinced they had taken my good paint horse.

Now, I was always a hearty eater but this morning breakfast just didn't look good at all. After all, this young cowboy had just lost his prize horse and my appetite was gone. Now Granny was a good cook for sure. The long table that seated the crews during hay season was always piled high with fried eggs, homemade biscuits, sorghum, thick brown gravy, sausage or bacon, fresh butter, and sweet milk. A man couldn't eat no better that was for sure. If you left her table hungry, well it was your own fault.

Later after everyone else had themselves a hearty breakfast, I helped carry the dirty dishes into the small cook room. I just happened to glance down into the wood kindling box that sat beside the stove and that's where I found old paint. Yep, it was him alright, he had all the markings. He was a piteous sight to behold. Someone had sure busted him up bad; now all he was fit for was just kindling. It kinda dawned on me all of a sudden where all my prime riding horses had been going. Later outside, I let Joann in on my suspicions about who the horse thief really was. Now all we had to figure out was how we were gonna get even. That wasn't gonna be easy, the thief was a lot bigger, smarter and stronger than we were and we sure couldn't challenge him to a stand up fistfight. Problem was, RC was sneakier than we were, yep we had us a problem for sure. One thing was certain though; I was hardheaded and bound and determined to come up with some scheme to get even. I sure thought a lot of that paint horse. Shoot, the Lone Ranger hung horse thieves, but for the life of me, I couldn't figure how to get you know whose head in a noose.

One thing was certain; we had to be sneaky, real sneaky whatever our scheme was going to be. Well we never really got even with RC, it wasn't for lack of trying, truth of the matter was, he was just plain smarter and sneakier than we were. We did learn one lesson the hard way though, a cowboy only needs one horse and if you ain't got 'em they can't steal 'em. That little episode put us out of the horse business for good. From that day on, we only kept one horse apiece to ride. After that until I grew a little and was big enough to start getting kindling myself, we watched with a smile on our face as RC walked off to the bottoms after kindling. I reckon that was as close as we ever came to getting our revenge for poor old paint.

Friday night came and it was a prime night to go hunting. It was cold and frosty, but not a bit of air stirred and it was dark as a dungeon outside. George Dunn came a roaring up in his old truck, his hounds barking and bellowing, trying to wake up every living thing in hearing distance. Pa had his shoes on and was out the front door before you could say Jack Spratt. Our hounds surrounded the truck and were excitedly helping out with the noise and ruckus when me and RC arrived on the scene. Mister Dunn did have some good-looking Bluetick hounds. Now, they weren't near as pretty as them Walkers those boys brought down from the city, but they were big, long eared dogs, and they were tough as boot leather.

Quicker than a blink, we had our lights loaded and we were ready and itching to head towards the bottoms. I'll tell you now, I liked coon hunting, maybe even better than eating. It kinda gets in your blood. With all the noise and commotion going on around the place, I figured those coons would hear and know what was good for them. They'd lite a shuck out of the bottoms before we could get ourselves down there.

Now in actuality Rover was a cur dog. I never told him that to his face cause I didn't want to hurt his feelings. For some reason a bunch of hounds will jump on a cur dog and fight him, sometimes even kill him. Now that don't alter the fact old Rover was as good a coon or squirrel dog that ever ran the woods, but he smelled like a cur. Pa didn't want to take the chance of them Bluetick hounds jumping on him.

"RC, tie old Rover up, we'll leave him home tonight." Now, I know Pa hated to leave Rover behind but he just didn't have any other choice. Those dogs of George Dunn's were bad to the bone. Those suckers would fight at the drop of a hat and we didn't want them to have any excuses. I've seen them things fight each other when they didn't have anything else to jump on. They were mean alright.

Rover took it all in stride; he never let out a peep as we all walked away towards the river. I looked back once and he was just sitting there beside the house. Maybe he knew something we didn't.

Thirty minutes later we had one burning up the river as that coon made a hasty retreat north. Man what a racket, I swear them folks in Milburn eight miles away could hear them dogs a bawling if they had been listening. Sure was pretty music, better than the Grand Old Opry I got to listen to one time when we were visiting my Uncle Russie Dennis in Milburn. We all stood there a listening to the race, and to Pa and Mister Dunn arguing about whose dog was in the lead and which dog would tree first.

I noticed RC stiffen and turn his ear towards the race. "I'll tell you who's in the lead, it's Rover."

Sure enough, I heard his familiar yip yip. RC tossed his twenty-two to Pa and he lit out of there like his pants were on fire. Rover was fixin' to tree that old ringtail and if'n I wasn't mistaken there's where the fight was gonna take place. I took off after RC with Tim and Charlie Dunn, but trying to stay up with them older boys was like a turtle trying to outrun the jackrabbit that everyone always talked about. Funny thing, for some reason when I was doing chores my name always seemed to be linked to that turtle.

Sure enough a few minutes later I heard Rover tree and the other hounds run in on him. They circled a little bit back to us so RC was almost to the tree when I heard the fight break out. I could tell from the snarling and growling and RC hollering that Rover was in deep trouble. I shook my head wondering how in the world he got himself loose from his chain.

Running as fast as I could, I arrived out of breath just as RC was kicking the fighting dogs off from Rover. RC knelt down and called to the big red dog but Rover was scared and mighty chewed up. He ducked around RC and took off back towards the river with them Bluetick hounds in hot pursuit. We all knew if they caught Rover, he was a goner for sure. Even Quane and Fanny who Rover hunted with all his life had been fighting him, almost like he was a complete stranger to them.

RC handed me the leads to our other two dogs, then he took off in that long legged stride of his in pursuit of the dogs and Rover. Now Quane and Fanny together probably outweighed me by a good twenty pounds and I was really having myself a time trying to hold them. I finally laid down on the ground and wrapped the lead rope securely to my arm. If they were a going after the other hounds, they'd have to drag me with them. Which is exactly what they did for a few feet anyway. I do believe my one arm was longer than the other for several days. With enough screaming and then cussing like I had heard Pa do, I got Quane and Fanny cowed down enough to let me lead them towards the river crossing at a slow trot.

I wasn't there to witness it but RC told Pa and the rest of us, when he got to the river; Rover had his front legs across a log in deep water and was fighting the Blueticks off of him. Finally, Tim and Charlie Dunn dove into the river and bodily pulled their dogs back to the bank. Rover was scared and wouldn't come to RC who was swimming out to him. The last that was seen of the red dog, he was swimming down river away from the Blueticks and us. RC said it was a sad sight as he paddled out of sight in the dark. I just knew he thought we were all against him. Nothing could have been further from the truth.

I took Quane and Fanny on home and told Granny what happened, while Pa and RC scoured the river for Rover. We had no way of telling how bad he was hurt, but with five big hounds tearing at you we knew he was chewed up pretty good. Late that night they came in tired, beat, and cold, finding no sign of Rover.

Next morning we finished our chores then caught up our horses and headed out. I know Pa was figuring and hoping that Rover would be on the porch come morning. You could see the disappointment in his face as he came in and sat down for breakfast.

I'll tell you for sure it was cold that Saturday as we rode the bottoms on both sides of the river but found nothing. We looked high and low. I called until my voice box up and froze shut, refusing to utter another word and I was one of them kids that enjoyed talking. It was so cold I couldn't feel the reins between my fingers.

Pa came to us about dinner and ordered us to the house. He didn't follow us nor did he come in for dinner. That night Granny saved supper for him, as it was good and dark as he rode up to the smokehouse and unsaddled his horse. Shaking his head sadly, he sat down at the long dinner table and picked up his coffee cup. I knew he was deep in thought as he didn't even bother to saucer his coffee, just sat there sipping on it. Now any true blooded Oklahoma farmer always saucered his coffee before he drank it.

Me, Joann and RC finished milking and we were helping Granny wash, candle, and place her eggs in the egg crates when Pa entered the house. We all knew what that dog meant to him; well I guess I mean what he meant to all of us. He was just like family.

I hit the bed that night figuring on ways to exact my revenge on Mister Dunn's Blueticks and I can tell you I meant to do it. This wasn't the first time they'd caused me misery, no sir, several times I'd been out hunting and them dogs put me up a tree with Toko grasped firmly in my hands. I'd of shot'em for sure then but Pa would have been a little upset. I sure would have saved old Rover a lot of pain and misery if I had.

Well anyway, after the breakfast milking Pa rode out again. I could tell his old horse didn't want to go and I don't blame him, that west wind was blowing hard and it was icy cold. I knew Pa was gonna be cold. Back then, we didn't have the warmest of clothes to wear, not like today.

Me and RC left out on foot but we had chores to do first. Again, it was way past dark and milking time when Pa rode in. There was no use to ask, he hadn't had any luck. RC looked over at me and shrugged. We both figured Rover drowned in the river and probably was swept away downstream.

I don't know what kept Pa going but something did. Love for his dog, an instinct Rover was still alive, or maybe he just couldn't bear the thought of losing his friend. I don't know, but whatever it was Rover lived because of the faith in the farmer. Sure enough, he brought Rover home on the third day of his search. A little worse for wear, those Blueticks hadn't done him any good, but he was alive. Granny got out her needle, thread, and went to work. Yes sir, those hounds of Mister Dunn's chewed him up pretty bad but the fire was still in his eyes so I knew he would live.

Later that night with Rover lying comfortable beside the stove on one of Granny's quilts and Joann hand feeding him, Pa told how he had come across the dog. He explained how he was riding alongside one of the sloughs that led to the river about two miles from the house, when he had heard what sounded like a dog whine. Peering down into the jumble of brush and briars, Pa said he couldn't see anything.

Dismounting he slipped and slid down into the slough and pushed the maze aside and there laid Rover. Almost dead, somehow he smelled or heard Pa and whined the best he could to his friend. Pa said he had a heck of a time getting the heavy dog back up the steep muddy bank and over the saddle.

I looked over to where he lay beside the warm stove. Joann had covered him up with another quilt and was mothering him. He seemed to be enjoying himself but I knew he had to be in a lot of pain or he wouldn't have stayed in the house. The only times I ever knew Rover to come into the house was during a heavy thunderstorm or when we were shooting off firecrackers.

Well two months passed and Rover was back to himself and working again. He had lain on the front porch all that time too weak to get up. He was always alert and watching, as Mister Dunn passed by the house in his wagon, on his way to check on his cows or put out salt. Every day a Bluetick hound followed the wagon, just one. I never did figure out why only one accompanied Mister Dunn as he had five or six of them mean things hanging around him most of the time. As Rover mended, Pa took to tying him under a shade tree unless he was bringing up the cows or hunting. Then one beautiful spring morning a peculiar thing happened, it took me a while being a kid and all to figure it out. Mister Dunn rumbled up the road headed for his pasture and alongside the wagon trotted one of them Bluetick hounds of his.

I was gathering kindling and looked up to see Rover come out of the front door, and he was wearing a brand new collar. That thing was wide enough to cover most of his neck and it had two big rings riveted into it. Nope, this weren't no tie him up with collar no sir, I wasn't that green. It was a genuine dog-fighting collar, designed so them Blueticks couldn't slash Rover open again.

I grinned to myself as I watched Rover standing at the door. His eyes were glued on that hound and the hair on his back a foot tall, well maybe not quite a foot, but he looked downright peeved. This was gonna be a real tussle if what I thought was gonna happen, happened. Rover wasn't standing there like a statue for no reason; nope, I could see the rope that was holding him back from where I stood. Now I knew why Pa had kept so quiet, never saying a word as Mister Dunn's dogs had been crossing our place almost every day. Yep, he had been scheming himself, now all that thinking was fixin' to be used. I didn't think he'd let them sorry hounds almost kill his favorite dog and not do anything.

Closer and closer the wagon came until it was almost even with me. Suddenly from out of nowhere, a red streak passed my eyes and Rover hit that Bluetick like a cyclone or tornado. Now I never ever seen a real cyclone but I heard they were jim-dandies at tearing things up. I had to hand it to Old Blue, he would scrap; well he did for a few seconds. Poor thing didn't know what was eating on him, a crocodile or a bobcat. Now I figured he never saw a crocodile so it had to be a bobcat he was thinking on.

At first, he fought, then he tried to run, then he ran under the wagon growling and finally he fell on his back screaming in terror. I looked up at the house to see if Pa was gonna come out and break up the fight but he was nowhere in sight. Course now something done caught my attention in the window, a curtain moved a little as I peered at the house.

Now you'd think with all the chickens squawking, the other dogs setting up a commotion from the ends of their chains, cows trying to jump out of their pens, and horses running to the far end of the stomp lot, surely somebody would have heard the ruckus and come outside. RC, Joann, Granny, and Pa were all inside, leastways they were when I walked outside, but not one of them put in an appearance. I sure wasn't about to endanger my life and limbs by getting between them dogs. Shoot either one of them outweighed me, besides Rover was winning.

I could tell by the way Mister Dunn stood up, he was thinking on jumping down and helping his dog, but I guess I don't blame him for changing his mind. Rover was normally a gentle, sweet, lovable dog, not today, no sir. To say the least, he was a little riled and out for revenge, and listening to the way that Bluetick was carrying on and hollering, he seemed to be getting it. I wasn't about to interfere even though I knew exactly what that hound was going through, I'd been there myself a few times, that's not quite right. I should have said a lot of times.

All of a sudden, Pa rushed out from the back of the house like he was all out of breath and hollered at Rover who retreated to the front porch. Apologizing up and down to Mister Dunn, Pa had a smug grin on his face as Mister Dunn clucked to his team. The wagon headed for the river with the Bluetick lying in the back cowed down and a little worse for wear. Well, it could have been worse, the hound leastways did get to ride in the wagon, he didn't have to walk today, probably couldn't anyhow. Now I ain't a saying Pa deliberately sicked Rover on that hound but things looked kinda fishy. Like my Daddy use to say, if something smells fishy and looks fishy, it must be fishy. Well anyway, Pa had a smile on his face and Rover was strutting around like a king or something. Granny wasn't smiling though, I reckon that little set spooked her chickens so bad they didn't lay for a week. Cows didn't give much milk either that night. Our hogs were a mite excited and nervous, but nothing ever kept them from eating.

Now I'll tell you, my Pa never had an ornery streak in him at all. Wish I could say that for RC, but it was a fact you just didn't mess with one of Pa's dogs either, especially Rover. Funny thing about the whole deal, from that day on I never seen not one of Mister Dunn's hounds following his wagon across our place, which was mighty peculiar.

Well anyway after that Rover wore that collar for almost a month and from time to time he'd come home looking kinda tuckered and a little frazzled. Pa would only laugh and pat him on the head. I reckon before the whole deal was finished, every one of them Blueticks took a licking from that big red dog. Those dogs wouldn't even run across our farm hunting, I guess they just didn't feel welcome on our land anymore. I heard Tim Dunn tell RC one night as they were smoking out behind the smokehouse that those hounds of theirs seemed scared to leave the yard.

After that, the big collar went into retirement and I guess I never seen Rover fight again. He was just a big lovable dog but on our farm, he was the master and he was treated like a king. He fed us, worked for us, and when you were down and needed a friend, he was always there to comfort you. He deserved the best because he was the best.

Chapter 9
The Bobcat

It was spring, kinda warm out, and raining. Everything was sopped to the breaking point. Even the fish were tired of it, but not farmers, they never complain about rain. I did though; my mouth was forever running off, griping about the rain or something, shucks you can't do much with rain coming down in torrents. Now RC never said much one way or the other. He weren't no farmer either; I knew soon as he got old enough, he'd light a shuck out of there, leaving that farm like a scalded dog.

Wynona and Sylvia had gone off to the city and found themselves some city fellers to marry. I believe Sylvia caught hers down in Texas. Funny thing though, they always said everything is bigger in Texas, but he was just a little feller. Joann was still too young to marry but it would have been alright with me if she had. You see, Joann was quite a bit older than me, also taller than me, and she always had to have her way when we rode one of the horses. She always wanted to ride in the front where I couldn't see anything, and that peeved me to no end. Now today she won't tell it like that, but it's the truth. Can you imagine having to lean out and look around her all the time? Granny always warned us not to run the horse when we went to get the mail or anywhere else. We didn't run the mare at least until we were out of sight of the house, then we would turn her loose.

Kinda like the time Joann and me were riding RC's little black mare down in the bottoms. We had that mare flat out running when we came up on a double dip that was pretty deep. We made the first one alright but the second dip wrecked us. Joann pulled me off the mare and scattered us all over the bottom. She'll deny that too of course but it's the gospel. We weren't hurt but we had us a dilemma. Joann could boost me back on the mare that was nice enough to wait on us instead of running back to the house; trouble was we couldn't get her back on.

If we came walking back to the house afoot, Granny would know we fell off and that meant we had been running the mare. Yep, we had us a small problem that wouldn't have come about if Joann had let me ride in the front and walk the mare like Granny told us too. Rover stood off to one side looking at us like we had lost our minds.

We finally found a stump and got Joann back aboard, so everything turned out alright that day, but there were always others.

Like I said, it was spring and it was raining. Me and RC were horseback, I don't know where we had been, but we were both soaked to the skin. We might have been up to Wilson Shico's farm for breakfast that morning. Wilson was a Choctaw Indian, almost like kinfolks, and one of the nicest men I ever met. His wife Pearl was indeed a great lady and a great cook to boot. I remember that part sure enough, as a young boy I seemed to stay hungry all the time. That booming laugh of hers could be heard clean to Milburn, but they were the greatest folks. Anyway, she was a fine cook. That little kitchen of hers was so small and she cooked on a wood stove like all of us did back then. It was so hot in that little room, we'd sit there eating with sweat running off our foreheads, but did we ever enjoy it. You never left her home hungry.

Here we were sitting on this knoll overlooking the dirt road or I should say mud road, wetter than a dishrag, when what comes along but a big old shiny automobile splattered with red clay off our fine county road. Well for a fact, we were all eyes because we sure didn't see many cars in our part of the country and none as big and shiny as this one was. Low and behold, the thing turns down the lane to our farm.

Now I figure RC already knew who was in the car, just wasn't saying anything. He never would tell me nothing, I knew he thought I was just a dumb kid. Now I wonder why? Withholding knowledge from me was the very thing what kept me ignorant of the facts. RC shook his head as the car proceeded slowly along the lane leading to our house. I could tell he had his doubts to whether that muddy road was gonna hold. That old dirt lane would hold up a wagon and team of horses but I wasn't so sure it was constructed to hold up that huge automobile. I figured that was exactly what RC was thinking as he watched closely, his eyes fastened on the road.

Sure enough that new shiny automobile was rolling along one minute and the next thing we knew it just sunk right there in front of our eyes. Man what a sight, mud was up around the doors and the people inside had their heads hanging out the windows looking dumbfounded at the ground. Weren't no need trying to back that thing out, cause as the man said when he fell in the pigsty, he was mired.

We rode on down the hill to where the car sat with its brand new shiny hubcaps buried clear out of sight. It was my Aunt Wynona and her husband Howard up here from Texas. Their little boy Mike was in the backseat sound asleep and missing out on all the fun. Now I got to hand it to Howard, he didn't seem too worried or upset about the situation. With his brand new car buried clear to the doors in mud, he never uttered a word. If it had of been my new car, I'd sure been doing some yelling, having a fit or something.

After everyone baled out of that beautiful car, or as it turned out climbed out the windows, they seemed to take turns walking around it shaking their heads. Not me, no sir, I sat right there on my little quarter horse mare Trixie. There weren't no need me getting myself all muddy, not that I was allergic to mud or anything like that, but facts were facts. They were stuck up to their eyeballs in black land mud and they sure weren't about to be going anywhere fast.

Well after all that looking and head shaking everyone came to the obvious conclusion, which by the way I had figured out before they abandoned the car. They were fixing to walk the rest of the way to the house.

Well I had to get off my horse anyway as RC gave me that long scowl of his and motioned me down. Not that Wynona hadn't grown up in mud and barefooted most of her short life but she sure wasn't about to admit it in front of Howard. The way she was tiptoeing around in front of him, she acted like she had never seen the stuff in her entire life. Trixie my little mare was young and she wasn't that well-mannered so I was a little apprehensive as we boosted Howard across her bare back. With a little coaxing and a few whoa's we managed to deliver our cargo safely to the house.

This wasn't Howard's first time down on the farm but it probably was the first time he got his brand spanking new car sunk hub deep in blue bottom black land mud. What was worse, it wasn't looking like the rain was gonna stop. Yep, the sky opened up again and it turned into a real frog floater for sure. Anyway, here I was, trudging along through the mud leading Trixie, mumbling and grumbling under my breath. I sure was a thinking it was dumb of them to drive off into that muddy lane to start with, but with a few hard glares from RC and I kept my opinions to myself.

After depositing Howard and Wynona into Granny's smiling arms, we had to return to the scene of the abandoned car and retrieve their baggage. You know, I've studied on it some but I could never understand why people had to bring every shred of clothes they owned to come for a weeklong visit. Shucks, they probably had more clothes in their littlest bag than I owned all together including my heavy coat.

Now like I said, Trixie wasn't just real gentle and she had a nasty disposition to boot. Them funny looking bags were about to eat her, and RC was about to lose patience with her, which meant things weren't going well. The closer he came to her with them suitcases, the more that little mare rolled her eyes and run backwards.

Well a couple of them bags landed plunk in the mud but by and large, we managed to get them all back to the house in one piece. While we were gone Joann snatched little Mike up and man was I happy about that. You see, Joann always wanted someone to baby-sit and Mikey fit the bill perfectly. When I was young, I always had to play dolls with her in order to get her to ride with me, as Granny wouldn't let me go alone.

Guess she didn't trust me when I was four or five years old. Now I hate to admit playing with a doll. Man I loved to ride and I could be bribed, but remember I was young back then. Now that I'm older and have my own horse, it is good that Joann had Mikey to play with, which let me off the hook, at least for awhile.

Like a miracle, the sun came out bright and warm the next day, so right after breakfast we all walked back down to the car with our shovels. Sure enough, just like I figured it hadn't moved one inch, it might have even sunk lower if that was possible. Well we dug and pulled mud away from the car so at least we could get the front doors open. Then we started on the back tires, like I said, I wasn't exactly what you'd call lazy. On the other hand, I didn't like to expend a lot of energy unless it was hunting. That car was mired in the mud, shucks even I could see the futility of trying to dig the thing out.

We finally had them back tires clear alright, but the problem was the bottom of that car was flat against the ground and it weren't gonna budge one inch. Howard climbed in and tried to back it out, only to have them rear tires spin like a top when it hit the ground. Yep, just as I thought, she weren't going anywhere. Pa stood back and removed his old felt hat then scratched his head. It sure wasn't looking good; it was time to get the horses. Our work teams were powerful animals but I still had my doubts that they could pull that heavy car out of that mud. Now I weren't no mathematical genius, but them horses only weighed one ton or a little more together while I heard Howard tell Pa the car weighed better that three tons. Now that didn't seem like a fair match to me and that ain't taking account of that black mud. Man that stuff stuck to everything like stink on a skunk.

However, Pa assured Howard if we could just get the car a little bit forward out of the bog hole he drove into, the car would be able to make it on to the house. Pa had RC go to the house and get Coaly and Lou and several chains. I couldn't figure why we needed so many chains, weren't no need chaining the car up, cause it sure weren't gonna run off by itself.

I knew one thing for sure though; we were going to need more teams of horses. Anyhow, by the time we got back to the car, Howard and Pa had cleared the front tires and what mud they could of the underside of that Packard. Yep, that's what it was called a Packard, and from what Howard said one of the heaviest cars made. The team of horses had their ears cocked forward and were really looking that shiny automobile over, I'll bet they sure loved to hear that little bit of news.

Pa hooked Coaly and Lou to the front bumper of that big automobile and I retreated out of the line of fire. Well he clucked to them as I watched from my vantage point as them old trace chains tightened when them big horses leaned into their collars. Nothing, zilch, strike two, that car only leaned forward a bit as that team pulled for all they were worth. Finally, Pa hollered whoa and stopped them before they strained themselves or broke something.

I knew it; I looked over at RC and quickly forgot the grin I was fixin' to put on my face. Unhooking the horses, Pa with us following proceeded to withdraw back to the house, kinda like a strategic retreat. In other words, that car whipped us soundly the first two go-rounds. Pa was as proud of that team of horses as he was his dogs, when they couldn't wiggle that old Packard, he wasn't happy.

Sure wish I had of been thinking, I could have won me some marbles on that little fiasco. As lucky as RC was, if I had of bet against them, the horses would have walked right out of there with that car slicker than boiled okra going down.

We had our biggest team of horses harnessed already, the rest of our teams were lighter horses without the pulling power of Coaly and Lou. Pa sent RC to Wilson Shico's farm, he had a big team of mules and we were gonna need'em. That Packard was one up on us but Pa wasn't beat by a long shot. No Sir, as I learned in school some navy feller said; we had just begun to fight.

Pa sent RC after Wilson Shico and his team of mules, so while we waited for him to return, we harnessed Bill and Nail. I could have told Pa that Old Nail was a waste of time, shucks she was lazier than I was. Dragging two triple trees behind the two teams, we started back for another go at that Packard. I could tell by Howard's face, he wasn't too sure of the attack we were fixin' to mount on his brand new fancy car. Pa was determined, Howard was anxious, and I had my doubts. Howard had to be back at work in a week or so and that car was his ride back. I figured right then and there, poor old Howard would be spending all of his vacation trying to dig that car out.

An hour later after considerable more mud digging and finally getting four horses and two big mules hooked to that stubborn automobile, Pa was satisfied and ready. He had his hat pulled down tight, his jawbone was thrust out, and I'm a telling you, he was determined. Myself, I was wondering if that thing they called the bumper would stay hitched to the car. Now I wasn't worried about Nail doing too much pulling, like I said she was lazier than I am. I always got blessed with using her when we were planting corn. I can tell you for a fact, she didn't even like pulling that little old light corn planter. However, the rest of them animals could and would pull with the best of them. I reckon Pa only put Nail in there to give the others confidence.

Everything was ready; me and Rover stood off to the side and watched interestedly. I was on the verge of the marble bet again but I chickened out. If that bumper held, something had to give with all that horsepower hooked to the car. Trace chains and harness were rechecked, everything was ready. Pa nodded at Wilson and RC who held the lines and with a flip of the lines them horses leaned into their collars once again.

I could hear those bolts on that bumper groan as the car began to move. Them horses were straining, the muscles bunched in their hindquarters as they were inching forward. Them trace chains were so tight a man could have played a tune on them. Slowly, inch by inch, that Packard started to move, Pa laid the check lines to old Nail and she jumped forward and actually pulled her weight. That's all it took, that car slipped out of that mud like a greased pig out of a gate.

Rover barked a couple times in excitement and we all cheered. Howard checked his car over and thanked everybody present. I could tell he was relieved, the car was unscathed but it sure was covered in mud.

As we watched Howard head up the lane, Pa announced it was dinnertime so Wilson and Pearl hooked their team back to their wagon and followed us back to the house. Granny had a big dinner prepared and everyone was in a mood to rejoice, especially Howard who jumped a broomstick to prove it. Now if you think it is easy to jump a broomstick, hold one in your hands and try to do it sometime, but remember to have a doctor on hand in case you break your neck. Howard made it look easy but he was a very nimble and agile young man at that time.

One week later Howard and Wynona were headed back home after a great visit. Pa, Granny and Joann were on their way to California to visit their daughter and son-in-law, A.C. and Reba Dennis, my folks. That only left RC at the farm to take care of the place, do the chores, and go hunting, course now Rover was there to help out.

Despite milking fifteen cows, shelling corn for a couple hundred hens, gathering and cleaning the eggs, feeding half a dozen fattening shoats, and feeding twenty or so horses, RC had time to hunt and that was about the only pastime he had. This was way before television; radio was boring except for our favorite shows like the Lone Ranger, Yukon King, and Lash Larue. The women liked the Grand Ole Opry themselves, and of course Loretta Young.

Well the folks were gone, RC was his own boss and it was time to go hunting. It was coming on dark, Tim and Charlie Dunn arrived at the farm ready to go. This time the Blueticks were left home. Rover, Quane, Fanny, and one black and tan hound that belonged to Charlie Dunn stood anxiously waiting for the carbide lights to be lit. Off to the bottom towards the river they raced eager to be on the trail of old ringtail.

Now RC and the Dunn boys were young and full of energy, they could hunt all night and work all day. Already two hard races had been run up and down the river with the dogs treeing both times in trees where the coons were easily located. Again, the dogs were turned loose and after several minutes struck a hot trail. Down the river they went running hard, bawling all the way. Man what a race, whatever they were running was moving fast and hard. R.C was beginning to have his doubts, but Rover and Quane were straight coon dogs, they wouldn't run nary a thing but a coon. Leastways at the time, that was our way of thinking. I think RC began to have his doubts, whatever they were after sure wasn't laying down a track like a normal coon, but he wasn't saying a word.

Twenty minutes later and two miles down river Rover gave his tree bark and sat down. Quane pulled up right beside him and started treeing. All four dogs were bawling their heads off, knocking the roof out of that old tree that was just bristling with leaves. We took our time getting to the tree as them dogs weren't about to vacate the premises unless of course old ringtail left out first. Finally, arriving at the scene of all the commotion, everyone scanned the tree unable to spot their prey. Those dogs were setting up such a racket, we figured old Mister Coon had to be there for sure. Course now not seeing the coon was no big deal as carbide lights and kerosene lanterns don't just give out the best of light to see by and the dogs treed in a live oak tree covered with leaves. Now Tim was a climber, the best in these parts, so up he went, checking one limb at a time.

Somewhere up that tree was a coon and Tim was bound and determined to find him. Those dogs weren't lying, no sir, he had hunted with Rover and Quane half his life, up there behind them leaves somewhere was a coon. Tim was one determined Indian as he inched his way upwards, his carbide light giving out an eerie light as it shined its dim rays about from limb to limb.

Tim was about twenty to thirty feet up when his eyes lit up like one of them roman candles going off on the Fourth of July. Directly in front of him, not ten feet out on a limb laid the biggest bobcat he had ever seen. He said later that thing looked like a mountain lion lying there with his fangs bared, his ears flat against his ugly little head, and that sucker was crouched and ready to spring.

I bet that would make a man fainthearted alright, seeing all those teeth and claws sticking straight out and them yeller eyes spitting pure hate and no back door to escape through. Tim swore his claws and teeth had to of been five or six inches long, leastways they looked that long as he tried to decide where to go if the thing charged. Now me being a realist, I could have told him straight down was the fastest route. I don't consider myself a coward, normally if'n I get myself in a situation of life or death my heart is strong, but my legs do get a little nervous and know when to leave out without being told. All the dogs were bouncing around under the tree expecting a little old twenty-pound coon to come dropping in among them. About that time with all the barking and leaping at the base of the tree, everyone's eyes glued straight up, we were ready or at least we thought we were. Man, we sure were surprised when old Tim landed himself right in the middle of that pack of hounds, with that bad tempered bobcat just two jumps behind him. Yes sir, I'd say them dogs were a bit astonished themselves when Tim lit on top of them, not to mention that fifty-five pounds of angry bobcat. Now like I said before, that little old cat was all claws and teeth, he was riled, and he was in hot pursuit of poor old Tim who was trying his best to crawl and kick his way out from under them hounds. I mean he was on all fours, his feet and hands just a clawing the ground. Funny thing was, as hard as Tim was trying, he wasn't making any headway and those long claws were only inches away from his backside.

It seems up in the tree before Tim had time to make up his mind which way to go that old cat went and charged right at him. Didn't leave him much choice but to bail off that limb like a shot, launching himself right in the middle of all four dogs. Our dogs were used to a little old twenty-pound coon hitting the ground, which was normally an easy battle for four or five dogs. Full of confidence and without looking they waded right into the meanest varmint that walked the banks of Blue River. I reckon they were a bit surprised to find fifty-five pounds of teeth and claws waiting on them. Man what a racket, squalling, growling, hair and fur flying through the air and poor old Tim under it all screaming and hollering, begging for mercy, and praying. I don't know what he figured we were gonna do, I just stood there my mouth plopped open and my eyes blinking. Every now and then, you'd see one of Tim's feet sticking out from the pile. I figured he was a goner for sure. I can see the papers already, Indian eaten alive by a bobcat. I'll betcha that would have sold some newspapers. If it hadn't of been so dangerous it would have been comical. Poor old Tim was on his stomach on the ground, the bobcat was on top of Tim, and the hounds were all over both of them. I couldn't tell what Tim was hollering but he was definitely pleading for help of some kind. The bobcat was hissing and squalling, and those dogs were all growling and barking. While it lasted, it was a battle for sure but it turned out short and sweet, that bobcat went through them hounds like a dose of salts.

It was kinda funny though, from a spectator's point of view that is. Poor old Tim was a crawling on his hands and knees out from under that jumble of fighting dogs and that cat a hollering bloody murder. I reckon Tim done thought he was a goner for sure, I know I thought he was. To this day I can't believe he escaped without nary a scratch, after falling at least twenty feet out of that tree maybe more, then not getting bit by the dogs or clawed by that wildcat that was doing flips on top of poor old Tim's backside. For awhile there in the gloom of the dark, I thought the boy was being eaten alive, man what a racket. RC couldn't shoot the thing even though I knew Tim was praying for him to shoot something.

It didn't take long though, even Rover backed off with several long claw marks marking his sides, tackling that ball of fur was like taking on spring steel with razor blades for toenails. Seeing the dogs were taking a whipping and about to become mincemeat RC up and shot poor old Mister Bobcat with his twenty-two before he had a chance to turn one of Pa's dogs into supper or jump a straddle of poor Tim who was still crawling. I don't know how he missed the boy with that shot, but right about then I don't think it mattered much, Tim definitely needed some kind of assistance. At the sound of the shot, Rover went back in for the throat. With the heart of a lion, there was still a lot of fight in that little old cat but finally he gave up the ghost and bit the dust. I swear, when all that fighting and growling finally ended my eyes lids were popping like a frog's in a hailstorm. I'm telling you I never seen nothing like that melee in all my born days. It hadn't lasted long but with all the hollering, caterwauling, and begging for some kind of help, it sure was more exciting than when I found myself at the bottom of a fight in town. Those town kids were a rough bunch for sure but I believe that bobcat had them beat at being the downright orneriest.

The dogs hadn't taken a whipping yet but they were well on their way until RC and his gun stepped in to even the score. That little ole cat's claws were longer than his tail and his teeth sharp as needles. When they get serious and start to fight, them things are downright nasty. That wasn't even counting his size, this one was the biggest I ever seen. However, mostly it's the fight in them, they're downright mean when they get riled and they stay riled most of the time. Like the man said once. "It ain't the size of the dog in a fight; it's the size of the fight in the dog.

Well wouldn't you know it, as luck would have it, Pa and Granny returned from their trip a week later. No sir, that didn't give Pa's hounds any time at all to heal up from their encounter with Mister Bobcat. Now mind ya, I ain't saying RC could have prevented the dogs from fighting that cat, but he might have stopped it a little quicker if he had been a mind to. Course he might have shot old Tim if he had fired quicker but I'm thinking at that particular moment, Tim wouldn't have cared.

Quane looked like she'd been through a meat grinder. Rover had a few scratches but his long hair prevented him from getting it too bad. Fanny, well she always was a coward or maybe she was just smart. Anyway, she weren't about to get herself mixed up in this fracas other than stand back and bark a little. You might say she was the rooting section. Never did see the other hound that the Dunn's had brought, he felt one swipe of that thing's claws and he left that little fracas headed out for greener pastures.

As always, before breakfast and right after the milking was done Pa always checked on his dogs, especially if they hadn't come greeting him first. That morning they hadn't, nope nary a hound showed its face at the back door. That got Pa's curiosity aroused to say the least and that curiosity got itself itched. I can just see the look in Pa's light blue eyes as he looked over his prize hounds. They were indeed a pitiful looking sight, so stiff from the fight they could hardly move out from under the house to eat.

Back at the table, RC watched as Pa attacked his poached eggs. He was upset, real upset. I had never seen a person stab an egg before, but sure enough that what he was doing, right through the heart or yoke. Yep, Pa was upset alright, looked to me like he was madder than the bobcat was last week. Now I wonder why, his prize hounds were cut all to ribbons, so stiff that they could hardly walk; they were a sorry sight for sure. Shoot did you ever see one of them puzzles where you draw a line to the dots, that's what them dogs looked like. RC had greased them down real good and that only made things worse with dirt, leaves, and feathers smeared all over them. Well sir here it came, the truth and then the consequences, Pa was finished with them eggs, now it was poor old RC he was eyeing.

Pa looked long and hard down the table at RC then laid his fork down. "You boys do any hunting while I was gone?"

"Yes Sir." R. C. mumbled.

"Did you tree anything?"

Well everybody knew they had, Rover, Quane, and Fanny didn't miss treeing at least one coon each time they went. I was curious as to how RC was gonna wiggle out of this mess.

"Yes sir." I had to hand it to him; he wouldn't lie. Wouldn't done him no good anyway, all you had to do was look at them hounds. "What did you tree?" Now Pa wasn't about to hurry this questioning, he was bound and determined to drag it out instead of stating the obvious. It reminded me of a cat toying with a mouse.

"Few coons and one little old cat." RC admitted it, right up front. If'n it had of been me, I'd have tried to lie my way out of what was gonna be a good strapping for sure. Dang sure wouldn't have hurt anything to try.

"What kind of cat?"

"Just a cat." RC kept eating calmly. He knew what was coming so he figured to fortify himself with Granny's good cooking.

"This cat, did he have a short tail about so long?" Pa held up his hands.

Now RC has been hunting all his life and was practically raised in the woods. Pa was well aware that RC knew what a bobcat was and what one looked like.

"Yes sir, reckon he did at that."

Well that's all it took, I expect just a little while after breakfast RC knew what them dogs was feeling like as they lay up under the house. I always thought I knew what a man fixing to be hung felt like on his way to the gallows and that smokehouse sure felt like a gallows on several occasions. Now I ain't saying RC was innocent all the time but on this occasion, he was. Those hounds were running trash by treeing that cat and if they didn't know the difference, how in the world were the boys supposed to know. I'll guarantee you one thing, weren't nobody gonna get between that cat and them dogs with all the teeth and claws being used. No sir, it was every man or dog for himself and Tim Dunn will sure testify to that.

Well to make a long story worse, the dogs healed and lived to hunt another day. RC took his medicine and lived to hunt another day. That poor little old bobcat that wasn't bothering anybody, well it was curtains for him. Sometimes there just ain't no justice in this old world.

Chapter 10
The Rattlesnake

As the seasons roll by, winter goes and spring comes, then the long hot days of summer arrive. I for one was always happy to see the cold days and nights of winter slide by. Yes, you could call me fickle I reckon, when it was hot I wanted it cold, and when it was cold I wanted it hot. Anyway, we had a lot more work to do come summer but at least a body was warm and his teeth weren't chattering like a magpie.

Every year I worked the rows of Pa's garden and every year they seemed to grow longer and longer, and I wasn't that old. Problem was the older I became the more work I inherited and I figured I had my fair share already. One thing was for sure though; as long as it rained and the sun shined, we'd all have plenty to eat.

Now as you've probably figured out, I wasn't overly eager to go looking for something to do. Not Pa, he always had something or other to say about idle hands and mischief. Believe you me; he kept our hands from being idle. I have to admit though that didn't keep me from getting myself into mischief. Now, I always figured hunting, fishing, and stuff like that was work but not Pa, no sir, that was fun stuff to him. You ever tried to wrestle a forty-pound catfish out of the river, now that's work. You ever tried to run a coon down river afoot following those hounds on a hot summer night, that's work. Way I figured it, they have four legs, we only got two and that makes a difference, in my opinion which didn't amount to much back then, it's work.

Again it was early summer, we had spent a long day in the hay fields. It was the first cutting of the year and we were tired. We were all leaning back taking it easy and relaxing on the front porch after supper when we heard a car coming up the lane. You ever watched a bunch of geese craning their necks at something. Well that's what we all looked like trying to see who it was, like I said before, we didn't just have cars running up and down our old sandy lane. No sir, one a month would be pretty close to right.

It was the old Chevy sedan of Mister and Mrs. Wooten, longtime friends of Granny and Pa's. Before the car came to a rocking stop and the door swung open, Pa had the domino table set up and two coal oil lamps burning. Joann brought out a number three washtub and we started filling it from a rain barrel sitting under an eave of the house. The idea was to set the tubs half-full of water under the lanterns. When the little creatures of the night, like June bugs, moths or whatever ventured out to disturb Pa's domino game would fly around the light, finally making their big mistake and fall into the water. Anyway, that was the whole idea, sometimes it worked and then again, sometimes it didn't. If it didn't, well you always had flyswatters in abundance to work those little critters over with.

The Wooten's were the sweetest people I guess I've ever known, not counting Granny. They were good people and dear friends, and they loved their dominoes. At least Pa and Granny had a fighting chance against them, they didn't cheat like some I need not name. It was a beautiful Saturday night, warm and quiet out on the front porch. The river bottom was as dark as a deep well, only the call of the far-off whippoorwill sounded, disturbing the silence of the dark. Joann had her friend Francine over for the weekend. Now Francine was a piece of work, I stayed out of her way. She didn't tolerate my pranks at all. She sure didn't mind working me over when she got mad and it didn't take a whole lot to make her mad. She kinda reminded me of that bobcat.

Me and RC sat on the edge of the porch our legs dangling off the side listening to the rattle of the bones. Mister Wooten's happy chuckle was the only sound that could be heard over the occasional stomp of a hoof or the squeal of one of the horses as they laid their ears back when their hay was threatened by another horse or cow. Our old farm was definitely quiet that night. I could never understand how Pa could stay awake long enough to play dominoes after putting in such a hard day in the hay fields, but he did, he definitely loved his dominoes. I've seen him play all night and be fresh as a new picked daisy the next morning. He definitely had staying power. Now me, I was a cardplayer, we had a game back then called pitch, now that was my game. Dominoes put me to sleep, shucks if I got myself bored anything would put me to sleep, especially work.

We definitely put in a long hot day in the hayfield since sunup this morning. Pa looked fresh and wide awake as them old worn dominoes rattled around the table. RC thought about going hunting, it was a dandy night for it alright but I was tired and refused to go with him. For some reason, he didn't want to go alone. Normally he was glad to be shed of me, can't really say I blamed him. RC liked his quiet, he didn't talk much but he didn't have to, I talked enough for both of us.

Well, that left only aggravating the two girls, which could be dangerous or going to bed. Outside of hunting and work, there wasn't much to do down on the farm. We sure didn't have television back then. We knew better than to bother Joann or Francine, they'd go to hollering and Granny would be after us. Plus the fact Francine had a pretty good temper. Well we had just about decided to call it a night when I swear, another car with its headlights a blazing, tooted its horn, and came rumbling down our lane.

Two cars in one night, now, that was definitely a record for us. I was curious who this would be, we probably only knew a handful of people with cars. Alphie Rowland had a truck but he sure wouldn't be coming down our road, leastways not this time of night. Unless of course, he was going hunting or his dogs headed down Blue River and he was trying to circle ahead of them. Mister Rowland's hounds were a little trashy to say the least. They'd run anything with hair on it, no sir, they weren't particular at all. We weren't allowed to hunt with him, Pa said his dogs would ruin our'n, get them to running possum, skunks, and other varmints. Course now, we didn't say that to Mister Rowland, as we didn't want to hurt his feelings.

Pa must have had a good handful of dominoes cause he sure weren't getting out of his chair, no sir; he just slammed one of them bones onto that poor little table and hollered. I swear I could see the legs of that table bow a little, as his ham sized fist hit atop it. He did love his dominoes, especially if he was winning.

RC speculated it was George Dunn a coming up the hill and he was right. Mister Dunn had himself one of them little Ford Cars, black and square. Had itself a little jump seat in the back where folks could ride. Course now you better be on the skinny side if'n you figured to fit two people in that small space. I heard them boys of his say it was perfect to take a girl on a date, said they had to sit close. Never did figure why you'd want to sit that close to a dat burned girl, especially the ugly ones them boys took to the drive in picture show in Tishomingo. I'm telling you some of them girls were so homely they'd stop a time clock between ticks. I reckon it's like the man said though, love is blind, each to his own. I sure wasn't that blind and swore I never would be.

Sure 'nuff, that little black car rolled to a stop beside the Wooten's Chevy. George Dunn and his brother Jess extricated themselves and walked towards the porch. Pa hollered for them to light and sit, but as he had been with them all day in the hay field, he wasn't about to give up his winning ways just yet. Now if those old dominoes started to get cold, you betcha, Pa would have welcomed a slight break.

I could tell by the way them two men were fidgeting around the porch like they were in an ant bed that they had something mighty interesting to tell. Jess Dunn always smoked a pipe and tonight that thing was belching smoke like a freight train out of Durant. By now, me and RC were wide-awake and all ears. Rover had sashayed over to the trunk of that Ford and was sniffing around.

About that time, Pa hollered "Domino" slapping his last domino onto the table, and roared with glee. Standing up he walked to where the Dunn's were leaning against the porch. Greeting the two brothers, Pa introduced Mister Wooten who they already knew, then asked them if they were thirsty. Refusing, Mister Dunn apologized up and down, as he didn't mean to break up their domino game. He had one of Pa's pets trapped in the back of that Ford and he was wondering if Pa could get it out for them.

Now that was a curiosity in itself, if whatever was in that car was too mean for George and Jess Dunn to mess with, I knew it had to be bad. I automatically took a couple steps back as Rover smelled around that car, curious like. When that dog's hair stood straight up on his neck and he let out with what seemed like a worried growl, my hair raised up too, causing me to step back even further. RC grabbed me from the back and pushed me towards that car jokingly. I'm a telling you, by the smirks on them men's faces, I knew they were up to no good.

No sir, by then I done figured out what them two Dunn's had corralled in the trunk of that car and I wanted no part of it. Earlier in the day, long about dinner, Pa was hitched to the big buck rake just a rolling down that grass in rows for the loaders. All of a sudden, he whipped Coaly and Lou, and lickety split, outta there he came. He was moving like old Satan himself was hot on his tail. His eyes were big as saucers and he kept glancing back over his shoulder. By the time he got that team stopped beside where we were working at the old foot feed hay baler, he was white as a ghost. I'm a telling you he looked like he'd been rolled in a barrel of flour.

"Boys." Pa stammered, then pulled out his big blue bandanna and dabbed at his forehead. Man his hands were shaking like a leaf in a windstorm. "There's a rattler out there at least ten, twelve feet long."

Course now, with that all the men that were gathered about in hearing distance started to laugh; we had big rattlers in blue bottom but come on now, twelve feet long? I swear I thought he'd been hanging around me too long. Now I ain't saying I'd lie by any means but I was prone to stretch the truth now and again. Not this time though, I could tell by the look of him, no sir, Pa weren't a joshing us one little bit.

"I'm a telling you men." Pa seemed almost hurt that they didn't believe him. "That thing's head was almost level with my seat and I never seen his tail at all."

George Dunn laughed. "Carl, where 'bouts you got it hid."

"What?"

"The bottle you been nipping at."

Now everyone knew Carl Dennis was a tee tottler, didn't touch a drop. By the looks of him though, right about now would be a good time to start. "Let's go for dinner, give that thing time to get away."

Get away? Not George Dunn and some of the others, they wanted to find the rattler for his rattles and skin. Shucks a snake that big would be the talk of the county, make a man a hero, well anyway he'd probably get his name in the paper, leastways if he didn't get snake bit. Come to think of it, that'd put a man's name in the paper to. Not me, I done seen the look on Pa's face and I was headed for the house and dinner.

RC wanted to go with the others, but Pa wouldn't let him. Good thing for him, cause RC didn't have the brains God gave a goose when it came to a snake. Shoot, he thought them water moccasins down at the swimming hole liked him, they'd lay out in the water, their little beady eyes a watching our every move. They weren't my friends; I'd bust'em with a rock every time RC wasn't looking. All they were waiting around for was dinner, which I wasn't a hankering for it to be me.

I shimmied up the harness onto Coaly's back as high as I could get, hoping that snake couldn't reach my skinny little old legs if he showed his ugly face on the road. You can bet I was a watching each side of the road as we headed home. I could tell Pa was watching too, but not RC, he was just walking along behind the horses with an unconcerned look on his face. I'll bet if that old rattler had put in an appearance, he would have become a little more concerned.

We all stood looking at the car while Rover growled and pranced about it. The rest of our hounds retreated to the house to watch from a safer distance. When Mister Dunn reached for that trunk latch, the porch looked to me like a good vantage spot, so I beat it out of there.

The only thing them men had was a lantern to light the rear end of that car. Now I don't know if you folks ever tried to see by lantern light, but it don't shine far, and that's too close to whatever they had captured in that car trunk.

I could barely see what was going on but I could smell it was a snake and a big one. You ever get a good smell of a rattler; I'll guarantee you won't forget it. Anyway, George and Jess started dragging that monster out of the trunk and it was every bit of twelve feet long, maybe even longer. They slammed the trunk closed, then draped that ugly thing across the little car, making it sink a little lower. I'll take an oath, that snakes head or what was left of it touched the ground on one side and its tail dragged the other.

Kinda brought me up short as I looked at it, sure 'nuff made cold shivers run up and down my spine. Me and Tommy McGlaughlin was squirrel hunting awhile back and I stepped over a log across the cow trail. I swear that log moved, I told Tommy and he just laughed but we didn't go back to look. Man if that log was our dead friend here, he could have eaten both of us and still had room for dessert. This rattler laying out there just might have been that log. The day I seen the log or whatever it was, it were down close to the river, not far from the hay field and close to where it had been killed.

George and Jess left the snake laying there on the car, while they came up to the house for coffee and to do a little talking. They started telling how they'd been to Milburn and were on their way home when right in the middle of the road they seen him. Looked like a tree limb that had fallen from a tree but tree limbs don't wiggle.

First they tried running the car over him but that didn't work at all and that snake was about to get into the high weeds where they weren't about to follow. Now Jess wasn't above taking a nip now and then, mostly now, I could tell by the smell of him he'd been nipping tonight. All he could get his hands on was a single tree lying in the back seat, why a single tree was in that car I never figured out but apparently it was. Now George ran over that snake again while the snake was busy trying to flee. Jess piled out and started waylaying him with that single tree. A single tree is only a little over two feet long and they say a snake can strike their body length, depending on how energetic he was or how mad he was I reckon.

How Jess didn't get himself snake bit I'll never know, I reckon the man upstairs looks out for idiots and drinkers. Jess finally managed to whack that thing a few times and kill him. George laughed; he said Jess had swung at the snake several times before he landed a good one upside his head. Only thing I could figure was the snake smelled the whiskey and was afraid to bite Jess.

Anyway, they were gonna play a prank on Pa and tie the snake to the tongue of the buck rake that was still sitting in the hay meadow. The next morning when Pa raised the tongue to hitch up his team the snake would have come up out of the hay. It was a good thing they didn't, at that time Pa had a bad heart. That would probably have given him a heart attack and killed him deader than a doornail, right on the spot. Me, now I didn't have a bad heart, leastways not physically and I can guarantee you if that thing had come up at me I would have kicked the bucket stone-cold dead for sure. I almost did the time Pa sent me out to the stomp lot to look for his wallet. RC told me to look real good under the hay beside the wagon where they had been working. Well wouldn't you know when I swiped the hay around looking for the wallet there laid the biggest old Hog Snake this youngster had ever seen. Turns out, he was dead but everybody 'cepting me got themselves a good laugh out of watching me hightail it away from that wagon. I didn't see a thing funny in that little joke, reckon they did though.

Rover was pure poison to any snake; he hated them things almost as bad as I hated Castor Oil. I don't reckon I ever knew him to get bit, I figure he had but he never showed it. His long hair might have saved him. We had one of them snake worshiper churches down the road a piece. Me and Tommy McGlaughlin always wondered what would happen if'n Old Rover accidently got in that church and took in after them tame rattlesnakes. I'll guarantee there would have been a hot time in the old house that night. I'll bet them folks would have been talking in tongues for a fact. Yes sir, I bet them folks would have gotten religion that night for sure. Course now, when Pa got through with me, my pants would have been talking some themselves. Everyone knew Rover, what was worse everyone knew me and Tommy. Not that we were exactly bad, just a little mischievous. We studied on it for a few days but finally gave up on the idea. I'll bet it would have been a humdinger for sure.

Well, we let that idea slip through the cracks but we always had a backup plan for our next adventure. Kinda like the time Mister Lowe got himself tied in his outhouse by some unknown varmints, then they tipped the dang thing over sideways with its occupant hollering at the top of his lungs. I'll bet he thought a cyclone done up and landed on him. I don't guess they ever caught the responsible parties to that little caper.

They say when it rains it pours, and that year it seemed to pour rattlesnakes. Later on that summer, one of the grand babies was lying on a blanket in the yard while his mother was snapping beans on the porch. Every now and then she'd look the baby's way but as the baby was too small to crawl yet, it wasn't about to get away. Well the women were all gabbing as women do and the baby was sleeping contentedly as babies are prone to do, when all of a sudden the mother let out with a screech and fell over sideways in her chair.

The other women looked at the terrified mother then down at the baby and their blood run cold, their eyes got big as saucers and their hair must have turned grey. Right alongside that baby laid a rattler sunning himself. The baby was asleep and not moving but they knew if it moved in the least the snake would strike.

Hardly six inches separated the baby and the snake. There was no way they could get to the snake and kill it before it seen them, nor could they pull the baby from harm's way without stirring up the snake. They were all standing there in a trance not knowing what to do. The men were in the field and wouldn't be back until dinner. It was too far to send for them before the baby awoke.

Suddenly from around the corner a red blur flew by, grabbing the snake as he passed the baby. Rover had sensed the women's fear from where he had been lying under the porch and looking around to see what they were scared of, he spied the rattler. Leastways that's the way Pa explained it and that sounded good to me. You talk about the petting and loving going on, and a crooning over, well Old Rover got enough to last him a year, but he deserved every bit of it. He had put his life on the line again to protect his family.

Chapter 11
Pa's Garden Fence

Like I told you before, Pa had a garden the size of which most folks today would call a ranch. We also had us a rabbit problem that had to be solved. Those furry little critters were eating us out of house and home. You'd never believe how much one small rabbit can put away in a night. Early one morning I counted over forty in our garden eating everything they could grab. My idea was to just shoot them, but shells cost money and Pa said it would just be a waste of meat. No, we had to do something else. I sure wished my marbles multiplied as fast as those rabbits did.

I've always liked my sleep; sitting up all night chasing rabbits was not good for a young, growing boy. I mean, I had to be rested to learn my lessons in school. Something definitely had to be done about our over population of the little rascals. Now we couldn't expect our hounds to chase them little suckers away, as we had always wailed the snot out of them for running rabbits at night when they were little. Coon hunting was gonna be their contribution to our entertainment, so rabbit running was definitely out.

We definitely had to come up with another solution somehow and right about then is where the idea of the rabbit proof fence came to life.

Now that garden was huge, it was kinda like a mouth full of gristle; the more you worked and chewed on it, the more it seemed to grow. Pa sent RC into town to order him some of the new chicken wire he had seen around other folk's gardens.

Two weeks later, we got word our wire was a waiting on us in town so Saturday week found us on our way into Milburn loaded with eggs and butter. Just me and Joann rode in the back of the wagon as RC had other things to do. He did mention the word chores but got real nice and declined when I volunteered to stay and help. Now when RC didn't want you to help him work, and he was actually nice to you, he was up to something. I do believe I heard Abigail Baker from over at Emmet way calling. Anyway, when we pulled out for town there stood his little black mare standing hipshot in the lot, while all the other horses were turned out to pasture.

I studied on it more as I bounced on towards town and decided more and more that I was probably right. It didn't turn out too bad though, I set what I figured was some kind of a record with my slingshot. I hit one of Mister Dunn's Bluetick Hounds at, I'll bet, sixty feet. What a shot! That dog jumped like he'd been wasp stung. I pulled out my knife and notched me another place on the wagon but this notch was larger, yes siree bob, it was a humdinger of a shot. Joann, she didn't appreciate the fact that I was such a good shot; nope she just rolled her nose at me, jealous I reckon.

I prided myself on my marble shooting and on my slingshot accuracy. My fist fighting didn't rate that high. Most times, I wound up getting the worst of it. Granny would patch me up after almost every trip to town and then she'd ask me why I got into trouble with the town boys. I didn't tell her about RC and his fighting, course now I never knew him to get whooped. One thing I'll say about him, he was tough as old boot leather and he never needed patching up. I guess he got that way practicing on poor innocent little old me.

I remember one time, him and Leroy Armstrong got into it on the school baseball diamond. Well it was actually a cow pasture but we played baseball there anyway. If the ball accidentally landed in a cow pile, well that was an automatic double and no more, and that's what started the fight. A baseball hit by Leroy went smack, buried itself in the cow pile and right then they went to arguing who had to get it out. RC was the second baseman and old Leroy was the batter.

Now that thing was buried, you couldn't see hide nor hair of it. RC was I reckon in the tenth grade at that time. The boy was tall and skinny; I had to admit he didn't look like much. However, right there is where looks can be deceiving. I'll tell you he was strong as a bull and when he hit you, take my word for it; you knew you had been hit. He had them bony knuckles that could dot your eye quicker than a fat cow could switch her tail and on top of that, he was downright accurate with either hand.

Still, I didn't figure he could take Leroy who was muscled up like some of them Roman gladiators you see in books. Shucks, that fight didn't last long enough for me to warm up the ringside seat I had found. After the second lick that sounded like a sickening thud, Old Leroy said he had to go look for his cigarettes. Shaking my head in disgust, I dusted off my britches and went back to the outfield where they always put their worst players. I believe I could have lasted longer than that, I had on many occasions but I got to admit RC never hit me quite that hard.

RC wasn't exactly a troublemaker but it didn't take much to get him stirred up. I remember another time when he got into it, this time with Frog Murphy. I can't recall what they were fighting about but I knew I wasn't about to miss it. I was the first one out to the playground, finding me a good seat, high on a stack of bricks. I had what they called back then a bird's-eye view of the proceedings.

Now if Leroy Armstrong looked like a gladiator, Frog Murphy looked like Goliath. Poor old RC looked like a midget up against him. I had already bet two dozen of my ace marbles against the boy; this time knowing there was no way I could lose. Now it ain't that I'm not loyal, it's just what I called good business. I'm not joking, old Frog was about six foot six, probably weighed over two hundred, while RC probably didn't go over one fifty at best.

RC apparently found out I had been betting against him cause he glared at me as he walked by. A look that I knew meant trouble for me, providing he survived old Frog, which I doubted. Man, it was what I heard the men say about some of Rocky Marciano's fights, they called them a mismatch. We'd all sit around and listen to them on the radio but somehow old Rocky would always come out the winner. Those fights crossed my mind as I thought about it and worried about my marbles, not to mention my own good health.

Our two combatants squared off at each other on the old basketball court behind the school. Not a teacher was present; back in them days fighting was what kids did almost every day after school or at lunch. Teachers just didn't get involved but every red blooded, breathing kid that could walk or crawl was crowded around them bricks. Course now I ain't saying the teachers weren't watching, shucks everybody else was out there. Surely, they knew there was a fight going on; the whole dang school was vacant. They sure as the world didn't think we were all having a watermelon-eating contest. I'll guarantee they were watching from someplace around the school. Nobody in his right mind would miss the fight of the year. I'll guarantee you one thing, they were better than them Marciano fights on radio, leastways you could see them and hear the knuckles a cracking.

Anyway, the boys squared off and went at it. My wager was looking good, I swear Old Frog was turning RC every which way but loose. About then RC looked over at me with that look I knew so well and right then I knew my marbles were slipping right out of my pockets. The fight lasted a little while longer. Frog was manhandling RC and I was beginning to get my confidence back as Frog had him down and was hitting him with some good shots. Man it looked like a five-pound chicken smacking around a June bug. Yes sir, my marbles were looking safe again, I even thought about doubling my bet.

Next thing I know they're carrying my Goliath towards the school as limp as a dishrag. RC was brushing himself off then pointed his finger at me as he ran it across his throat. You know they say everything is fair in love and war. RC got hold of two bricks and when they came together, poor old Frog's head was right betwixt them. Kinda made me sick alright, no, not for Frog, he got what he asked for, should have moved his big head faster. Nope, I got sick a thinking I was about to kiss my marbles good-bye and probably my life once RC got me home.

Yep, it put old Frog's lights out right quick and there went my marbles out the window. Course now I didn't give them up without a fight. I argued that RC had cheated. Me and the feller I had bet with, Arthur Patrick went at it tooth and nail until RC broke up the fight and forced me to cough up my marbles. I figured he'd pounce on me after we got home but he didn't. I reckon he figured I had learned my lesson, losing my marbles and all. They carried poor old Frog to Mister McCleary's office where he was deposited on a couch, out cold as a cucumber.

Later me and Arthur went at it several times but I never did get them marbles back. You know they say you live and learn, well I'm still living but I never did learn much. I did learn one thing though that was the last time I bet against RC Dennis in a fistfight or any other thing.

The old wagon rattled on towards town, no other targets brought themselves close enough for me to waste a good river rock on, so I sat back and relaxed. Joann wanted to play Jacks; you ever tried bouncing a rubber ball on a rough wagon bed then try to grab them stupid little star shaped pieces? It's nigh on impossible, it was a dang girl's game anyway. I didn't want to play cards either, as she always beat me, I think she cheated but I never could catch her at it. Sure was a fine pickle I found myself in, Joann was smarter and RC was tougher, sure didn't leave me much. I felt like the little orphan whose folks moved away and left while he was still at the schoolhouse.

It was a boring Saturday altogether. Mary Peaster come outside with her freckles and pigtails and waved, her buckteeth shining like a possum in the moonlight. I beat it back across the street before some smart aleck said something and I had to bash his front teeth in. It sure seemed to me like everybody in town was trying to hitch me up with that woman. Now I ain't saying she was ugly, no sir, it ain't gentlemanly to speak out against a lady, let's just say well, she definitely weren't my type. I wish her and Jackson's bull could have met up face to face, I'll bet he would have left me alone after that.

Shucks, it was one of the few Saturdays we went to town where I came home in one piece. Most times, I looked like a jigsaw puzzle that someone had put together wrong, but not today. I think even Granny was surprised as she looked me over.

Can't figure what happened to them town boys, I reckoned they were off deviling some other poor soul. Well anyway, we loaded Pa's wire and I was a glaring hard at all them bundles of wire as I gobbled down another bologna and mustard sandwich. I just knew I was fixin' to be on the working end of that stuff stringing it around the garden. I should have just up and shot them rabbits; yes siree bob, that's what I should have done. Well I didn't and on account of them now I was gonna have to work.

Sure enough, Saturday we was all out putting up fence posts and stringing wire. I'd look off down towards the river from time to time, sure would be nice, shady and cool down there along its banks. Nope, here I stood sweating like a spotted lizard on a hot rock and for what. I missed my chance, should have shot them pesky things.

Well it took a few days but I had to admit we done a fairly tolerable job. That fence was tight and it was snug to the ground. I could just see them rabbits trying to figure out where they were gonna mooch their next meal. We all stood back nodding our heads and admiring our hard work. For once, even I was proud of the blisters I had earned digging those fence posts. Rover stood there wagging his tail and looking at the fence. Ain't figured what he was so proud of, he never hit a lick on the dang thing. I guess he figured he had guarded us from them ferocious rabbits. One thing was for sure though, I was gonna get me a good night's sleep tonight.

Pa traded for a young horse mule just a few days back. He was definitely a looker, big and kinda blue black, but he had that spookiness about him. You know what I mean, you ever look at a man that had a wild look out of his eye, waiting for him to explode? Well sir that was this blue mule. I ain't kidding you, he was a dandy, big and heavy as old Tom our other mule, but he had himself a mean eye on him, you know a little white around the old eyeball. Made me plumb nervous just waiting for him to make his move.

I knew for a fact, he had his mind on something besides work and I didn't want to be in front or behind him when he up and figured out what his intentions were. He was primed and ready, I knew he could and would kick like a Missouri mule if given a decent target, which wasn't about to be me. I was wondering who was gonna be the unlucky soul that had to lean over behind him and hook-up them trace chains. Weren't gonna be me, no sir.

We always led our teams to the smokehouse to harness them; it was a lot easier that way. Trying to lug fifty pounds of work harness across the stomp lot was just not too smart. Today Pa wanted us to start running the cultivator through the corn below the house before the Johnson grass grew any taller and took over, so here we were fixing to harness old blue. Roadie, Pa's mare mule was flighty at times but this one I figure would turn out to be a lunatic. We shouldn't have used her but Pa wanted to see how his new blue mule worked. Well he did alright, he seen him work. Worked us over is what he done.

The smokehouse just ain't real far from the garden and our brand new rabbit proof fence. R.C led old Tom and the blue mule over; don't remember what his name was. I remember what Pa was calling him that day but I won't repeat it now. Anyway, RC was standing at their heads and holding a cheek strap in each hand as I approached with that noisy harness.

Looking at that mule's wild eyes, you'd of thought I was a complete stranger and I was coming towards him with a grizzly bear under my arms. RC said to lay the harness on him real easy, that's what I was doing considering my head didn't reach hardly past his chest. Well, a little bit more maybe, but not much. Pa had taken a spell with his heart and had been ailing so he was sitting on the back steps watching the proceedings. He up and got himself an eyeful for sure, cause we sure enough proceeded. Man alive, we proceeded to tear down half the farm. What a show, almost beat the yeller horses performance, but not quite.

I already harnessed Old Tom, managed to get the collar on the blue mule, and buckled down. That mule was a wringing his tail and fidgeting around like he was standing in a red anthill as I approached with the harness. The closer I got the more that sucker commenced to roll his eyes and ring his tail, sure 'nuff made me kinda fidgety myself. I finally managed to get the hames squared away and buckled down around the collar but I don't know exactly what happened next. I sure found out what dynamite sounded like when it exploded, yep, the explosion happened real fast, right on top of me and RC

Pa later said one of the trace chains fell to the ground and set that confounded mule off. He was a pitching, kicking, bellowing, and trying to run all at the same time. Pa was a hollering whoa at Tom while me and RC was feeling of ourselves to see if we had any broken bones. Shucks, I just wanted to make sure I had all my parts still attached to me. I swear I had a hoof print square in the middle of my chest.

Yes sir, that blue mule had done knocked me backwards and run plumb smooth over poor old RC as he tore out towards the stomp lot. Now I never saw such a commotion in all my born days. Chickens were flying everywhere, calves were jumping clean through our pole corrals, and we had hogs running and squealing like they were being butchered. Not to mention every hound on the place were in hot pursuit of them run away mules.

I looked over at Pa, his mouth was gaped open and his blue eyes were batting faster than frog's eyes in a hailstorm. Right about then I was a wishing I had the nerve to let fly at that crazy mule with my slingshot but that might have been the last straw. Well wouldn't you know it, that team of mules circled the lot and headed straight for our brand new rabbit proof fence. I didn't figure they were gonna stop and sure enough they didn't fail me.

However, they did circle it. Right about then I breathed a sigh of relief, as I knew all our hard work was safe. I figured those mules would run themselves out and Tom would stop down there in the bottoms somewhere. Well it was just too much excitement for Rover and the hounds; they just naturally had to get in on the fun.

I don't expect ya'll know a whole lot about chain harness. The fact of the matter is them traces reach behind the mules and right on the end of each chain, for some reason they have a thing called a cleavis. It looks like two fingers curled at the first knuckle. Well anyway, them dogs fell in behind the mules and the team caught another speed. Wouldn't you know it, as they circled that fence, the cleavis pin reached out and took a stranglehold on that brand new wire.

Now a chicken wire fence don't stand much of a chance against two thousand pounds of runaway mules in a dead run. What a sight to behold, right before our very eyes. Poles, wire, staples, everything that was once standing was now strung out behind that team and headed due north towards the bottoms in top flight. I believe it took some of our tomato plants along with it as it passed.

Man what a wreck, RC never said nothing just stood there blinking and little old me was at a loss for words, first time I can ever remember that by golly. Even the big fire wasn't as mindboggling as what I just witnessed. I kinda knew what Noah felt like when he woke up and all the water was everywhere about his boat. Pa's mouth was still opening and closing but nothing was coming out.

I'll bet them rabbits were sitting out there somewhere laughing themselves silly. When things finally quieted down, we managed to capture the mules and lead them back to the house. They weren't hurt much, skinned up a little was all, but that fence, well it was past helping and that's to say the least.

Anyway, we was back to guarding the garden, I was never so sick of eating rabbit in my life as I was that spring and summer. Trouble was, I don't think we even put a dent in the rabbit population. They were definitely prolific little devils.

Pa had that blue mule shipped to a glue factory first time Roy Dobbs came by. Yep he probably made a nice big bar of soap; problem was, by that time the mule had done nearly bankrupted Pa. He done tore up more in a day than we could fix in a month, even if we had the money.

The chickens were so spooked they laid scrambled eggs for nearly a month and the cows, you rattle a gate and they'd jump out of the lot. Well maybe that's a little farfetched but I'll tell you it was a sight for sore eyes. It was a real show for sure; I'll never forget it, better than going to a Frankenstein movie. I don't remember it happening but that mule done up and kicked a bucket, I stood on to harness him, clean up into the old oak tree that shaded the place. I figure it's still resting peaceful up there.

Now if it had been me, I'd thought of someone I wasn't too fond of and swapped that old blue mule to him. Someone like Arthur Patrick, for instance. I had some real good dreams of that mule chasing old Arthur around the house till he give me back my marbles. Looking back on everything, it was kinda funny, leastways nobody got hurt and we had something to talk about for a few days.

Chapter 12
Mule Footed Hogs

Late summer was on us once again and it was crop gathering time. This was long before we had machines to pick our corn so we done it all the hard way, by hand. Now as I was the smallest, I got the dubious honor of driving the wagon and those hardheaded mules alongside the rows of corn. That was supposed to be the easy part, uh-huh. The rest of the family would pull the ears from the stalks and pitch'em into the wagon. Everybody got to participate, kinda like a family outing or something. By the sounds of it, my job seemed easy enough and it would have been if those contrary mules had cooperated a little bit.

Once the wagon was full, we'd drive it to the corncrib and unload and then back to the fields we'd go. Like I said, it was my job to drive the wagon, which suited me to the bone. Those old rows were long, so there were plenty of ears of corn to gather. It was hot and dusty, which definitely made for a long hot day in the field. Course now, every time we'd go by the river we'd take us a little dip and that would help cool us down considerably.

Here I sat doing my job driving them mules slowly up one row and down the next. Now, a nice juicy ear of corn is mighty tempting to a greedy mule and I never seen one of them long eared gluttons that wasn't greedy. It's a constant battle to keep their fat lips from latching onto every ear they could bite into. Here I am sitting up on that board seat a jerking and tugging on them mules and mind you, I weighed about eighty to ninety pounds. Each of them blamed mules weighed close to a thousand or better. Wasn't exactly what I'd call an even match in strength or weight. For once, I found a critter that was more stubborn than I was, come to think of it; they just might be smarter too.

Dad never was one to yell or threaten, no sir, he told me one time to do something and it better get done. Well, he told me not to let them mules grab them ears of corn and I was sure trying my best. They'd get one bite out of each ear then drop it as they tried to get another hold. Then they'd latch onto the next one they spied, like a tick on a hound dog. It was downright impossible to keep the dat burn things from grabbing an ear with each step.

Next thing I know Dad had done snatched me off that seat. I was a getting a good tanning with the end of one of those check lines, let me tell you them things smart. Now I was fuming, not to mention my backside was on fire. I couldn't sit down on that seat leastways, none too comfortable. I wasn't the one eating the corn; it seemed like to me as if those mules ought to be the ones getting the whipping.

Like I said, I was mad and I wasn't about to take another whipping on account of them hardheaded mules. Nobody thought to put a wire muzzle on them before we left the smokehouse, nah that would have made things too easy for poor little old me. Glancing behind me, I seen right away everybody was busy gathering corn so out comes my slingshot and I was ready. Well I did it, boy did I do it, when that inside mule reached for another bite and I let it fly. Uh-huh, wrong move, I'm telling you, oh I hit him alright and that's where the wreck took place.

That sorry sucker dropped his head and I swear he commenced to pitch right in them traces. I sat there bug eyed as that blamed ninny jumped as high as my head. Every now and then, he'd let fly with a hind hoof catching that old oak wagon right where my foot was resting. I dropped my slingshot somewhere under the seat and was hauling back on them lines as hard as I could, and hollering whoa, hollering, shucks I was screaming. Whoa, man he acted like he didn't know the meaning of the word. The other mule was sure 'nuff wanting to do something but I had his old head pulled round almost to his tail, all he could do was circle and take the other mule with him.

Dad was trying to get in the wagon when about that time the thing tipped up on its side and spilled the bed, corn, and me all out on the ground. I was hanging onto the lines for dear life when he finally got a hold of them and relieved me of that problem. The mule quit jumping around but he was still a bit upset and nervous. He was a ringing his tail around his hind side like a time clock.

Dad looked him over real good but he never could figure what happened. Never one to miss a good opportunity, I mentioned I had seen a wasp fly by just seconds before he started to act up. Well we got the wagon back together and were picking up the corn when Granny handed me my slingshot and shook her head. I guess she knew me pretty well, cause I never was able to get a good lie past her and I came up with some good ones at times. Now, I know you ain't supposed to tell fibs, but I'll tell you, stretching the truth every once in awhile sure saves a fellow many tail feathers. RC gave me a look like he wanted to choke me. Man, I'm the one that got the whipping, got flipped out of a wagon head first, could have been killed to death, shucks you'd think they'd feel sorry for me.

That must have been a pretty rough old wasp cause the next morning that dat burned mule had a goose egg on the end of his nose. A sore nose served him right, I had to stand up to eat for a couple days and I hadn't swiped any corn. Anyway, we had a good harvest, the corncrib was busting at the seams, and the hay was stacked higher than the house. Yes sir, we were living high off the hog, which reminds me of those mule-footed hogs.

You don't see'em much anymore, but years ago, a mule-footed hog was common. Most hogs have split feet, not these; their feet looked just like a mule's foot. They come out of them Arkansas Hills and they're meaner than the hillbillies that raise them, course I didn't know that at the time I became a proud owner of one. Five years back, we were up around Cloudy where my Aunt Jackie and Uncle George and their son Rowdy had a fair sized ranch. Well we were up there visiting and Aunt Jackie sent me home with one of those things. That sow was fixin' to have herself some little mule footed hogs, course now we didn't know that at the time either. I loved my Aunt Jackie dearly but I could have done without the hog.

We arrived back home and I could tell at first glance Pa was just tickled pink to see that long snouted, ridge backed, skinny, mule footed old sow turned in with his good hogs. He knew exactly what she was and I could definitely tell she wasn't exactly his kind of pork animal. Trying to eat one, you'd almost bend a fork trying to pick up a piece of sausage, that meat was so tough.

Uncle Brent and Uncle Buck my dad's younger brothers backed up to the mud lot we kept our hogs in, while Pa slid back the old gate. They had a truck and they volunteered to bring the sow to me. I always thought they didn't like me much and the way they were grinning at that sow, I was probably right. I'm telling you when that thing hit the ground, she hit running, right smack into that log fence she banged like a freight train. She didn't put on the brakes either, those corrals shook and trembled and I'll be dogged if she didn't head the other direction in high gear and did the same thing again.

The other hogs were all huddled in a corner, bunched up like flock of sheep watching that crazy thing run back and forth. I could tell they didn't figure that sow to be any relations of theirs. I just shook my head in shock, all this time I thought my Aunt Jackie liked me. Shucks, she just wanted to get rid of this idiot. I reckon that old sow's head must of got sore or she was trying to figure out some other scheme to escape. She finally found herself a corner and stood there eyeing us with them little pig eyes of hers.

Couldn't blame her though, we was all eyeing her right back. Pa, he wanted her in a smaller lot away from his good hogs, can't say that I blame him for that though, she was ugly, kinda reminded me of Mary Peaster. Anyway, RC up and climbs in there with her and I could tell right off that wasn't a good idea at all. That old sow was cat quick and meaner than a riled up porcupine.

Before his boots hit the ground, she was on him like stink on a skunk. I'm telling you that old sow meant business. Right about then, I done figured out I wanted out of the hog business and fast. RC made a hasty retreat over the fence and here we stood again all staring at one another. Pa was tempted to get his gun but fact of the matter, she weren't worth the powder it took to blow her head off.

I figured he didn't want to disappoint me in my first business venture so he hesitated to shoot the thing. No sir, it wouldn't of hurt my feelings at all. If we had only of known how much trouble, it would have saved us all. Pa called Rover in and opened the gate just enough to let him in. I'm telling you that sow came ripping across that lot like a mad bull. She was throwing dirt in the air and squealing. Then she'd stop dead in her tracks and go back to rooting at the ground.

Rover dodged out of her way a time or two, and then he made his move. That red dog latched on to her ear like a tick to a billy goat. Now they were pert near the same weight and the way Rover was chomping down on that hogs ear, I figured he'd rip it clear off. I've got to hand it to her, the old girl never gave up and she was game as they said back then. I had to admire her grit.

It were a tug of war for sure, they were a circling, around and around. She couldn't get loose to bite Rover and he couldn't maneuver her through the gate. Finally, RC baled over in the lot and grabbed her by the hind legs. With Rover controlling the front end, he controlled the back end. That only left one small problem, how were they gonna turn her loose and get the gate shut before she grabbed one of them.

Well, wouldn't you know it RC hollered for me to come close the gate. Me, shucks I'm the littlest one there but after all she were my hog, leastways for now she was. I was already figuring on who I was gonna swap her off to. Me and her was definitely gonna part company and quick. Well somehow, she got loose and escaped the pigpen. Rover didn't fool with the small gate he just cleared the fence. Amazingly all of us were in one piece.

I lay awake long into the night figuring out exactly how and when I was going to get rid of that thing. As it turned out all my worrying was for naught, leastways that's the way it turned out. The next morning we passed by the hog pen on the way to the milk lot and wouldn't you know it, she had up and escaped. That sow had done slipped her skinny carcass between two logs and vacated the premises. Hopefully she was headed due east back towards the mountains. Me and RC both grinned in relief. Believe me, we had no idea what lay in store for us next.

Old Skinny, that's what we called her, hid out down in Ballard Bottom or on our place but she stayed out of sight. Every now and then we'd catch sight of one of them things. Oh we'd find plenty of sign along the muddy banks of the river and every once in awhile we'd actually shoot one of them pesky little varmints. Trouble was, if'n they weren't young that meat was tougher than old shoe leather. Not that I ever had to eat shoe leather. I swear you could take a bite of that sausage or bacon and it would squeal at you. Well, maybe I'm stretching it a little, but that meat was tough, and it smelled to high heaven, man was it ever rank, it'd flat run you out of the house.

Anyway, I reckon about two or three years rocked by and we started running into more and more of her offspring. Now we never did till this day ever see Old Skinny again, but what the heck, they all looked pert near the same to me. I mean when they're coming at you at a run with their ugly snouts wide open they all look the same. On occasion, I did get a good look at some of them as I peered down at them from a low branch where they had treed me. I swear they were worse than Jackson's bull.

Most of them had a surly attitude about them. I swear it was getting downright precarious to go into that bottom afoot without dogs. Well, one fall day things came to a head. Pa had been squirrel hunting and we watched as he came limping back towards the house. Now right away, we could tell something wasn't exactly right as one of his britches legs was torn half off and he had a mad look about him, not to mention he was all muddy.

I was kinda hoping it was the bull again but I reckon I already knew it was them pesky hogs. It didn't take him long to get down to the matter. For once RC escaped scot free leaving poor little old me to face the music. Pa took me off to the end of the porch where me and him had us a serious discussion. You might say it was one of those Sunday come to meeting talks. Well anyway, whatever kind of talk it was, it all came down to one thing. Those hogs he considered mine, so they were my problem, and he wanted them gone or else and my little backsides would be the or else.

By the signs everywhere up and down the river, the hog wallows, the rubs, there definitely were more than a few roaming the woods. Taking in the fact that we hardly ever seen one unless they had run you up a tree, I just didn't know exactly what he expected me to do about this problem. One thing was certain though, falling back on my routine that I was just a kid wasn't gonna work this time. No sir, I had grown considerably, now he wanted them hogs gone and he meant it.

Dad was in California and I could tell right quick RC was enjoying watching me sweat and Joann, alias Emma Elizabeth, was a girl, no sir I was on my own this time. Oh, she'd listen to my problems, but she was still a girl, for once she didn't come up with one of her schemes. There was only one thing left to do; I needed me a hog man. I knew just who would know of one. Jess Dunn was my man, if anybody knew a man that could help me it would be him. It didn't matter, whiskey, women or song, I heard'em say, just call old Jess he'd fix you right up. Sounded like good advice to me, I had little choice, I didn't need whiskey or women, but I sure 'nuff needed me a hog man in the worst way.

Right after milking, I headed south to the Dunn's farm. I was a figuring all the while I was walking there had to be a way for me to come out of this deal with a little hard-earned money. I mean, after all I raised them hogs all this time. Well that was stretching it a little, but everyone knew they were mine. That's exactly what got me in this fix in the first place. I mean them hogs treed every hunter that came into Ballard Bottom squirrel hunting. For some reason, people seem to get a little upset when a crazy old boar hog chases them up a tree. Shucks, it was so bad I was getting me a real reputation, course now the squirrels and coons that were being left alone down there appreciated them hogs.

Well I found him, Jess Dunn that is, trouble was he didn't seem interested in seeing me, if he could see me at all and by the looks of him, I doubted it. I had done up and forgot the first rule of thumb when dealing with Jess was, make sure you talk with him before dinner.

Now Old Jess was a likable feller, yes sir, he liked his whiskey better than any man in the county. He could hold it leastways until dinner, after that he got kinda snookered, so they say. I'll say this for him; Jess was a hunter and a good one when he was sober. When we were on the track of some varmint, I never knew him to be tipsy. Granny didn't like me and RC hanging out around him much, so we kept mum when we went out hunting with him. However, this couldn't be helped, I needed me a hog man and I needed him bad. I didn't quite like the look in Pa's eyes when he said for me to get rid of them critters and be quick about it or else. I figured his or else meant; my backsides were fixing to get blistered.

Now I had smoked a vine a time or two but I steered clear of the spirits, not that I didn't have ample chances to take a nip now and then. We had some of the best moonshiners in the state practically in our backyard, shucks our family tree was full of them. For the life of me, I just couldn't get past the smell of it. Now my friend Tommy McGlaughlin would nip on it a little and he said it was pretty good. Just keep in mind he's the same feller that said Mary Peaster was pretty, must have been the corn.

Anyway, I started to leave, Jess came alive telling me to sit down, and we'd discuss getting rid of them hogs. Next thing I knew the subject of money came up. I kinda looked crossways at him, I didn't have any money, shucks I don't ever remember seeing much of the stuff. I watched as the tall man in the bib overalls fetched a pipe from his bib pocket and tamped it full of Bull Durham smoking tobacco.

As he struck a match and lit the pipe, he studied me through the plume of smoke that surrounded his head. Right about then, we got down to serious hog talking business, that pipe a blowing smoke and that bottle half full of Wildcat Whiskey all disappearing down his throat at the same time. Jess he had one of those oversized Adam's apples and it would kinda bob up and down every time he swallowed. I sat there and waited patiently, that's all I could do. I loved my Aunt Jackie, but along about now, I was mighty peeved at her.

Jess finally got around to the fact that he knew a man that could fetch those hogs out of the bottom and remedy me of my predicament. I started offering him a share of the hogs and then I offered him half those things. In the end it turned out I was almost gonna have to pay this man whoever he was to take the hogs off my hands.

This didn't sound right to me so I up and said my goodbyes and home I went. I got to thinking though, G.O. Jackson just lived down the lane and he was our county commissioner. Now if anybody knew a hog man it would be Mister Jackson, and as county commissioner it was probably his duty to come to the aid of one of his voters, not that I was old enough to vote, but I would be someday. Course now, I didn't figure on him still being mad about the bull and all. Before I managed to back my way out of his yard, I thought he was gonna sick his dogs on me for sure. Well that idea didn't pan out too well. After a week of asking neighbors and almost wearing the soles off my bare feet, not to mention the dark looks Pa was giving me, Old Jess' prices started looking better.

I couldn't blame Pa for being slightly upset. Shoot if you went into our bottoms hunting or anything, you better be a horseback and that horse better be able to run a pretty good lick. Those dat blamed hogs were getting meaner with every day that passed.

Back to Jess I went, we talked, we shook hands, and we had ourselves a deal. He assured me that he'd have his hog catcher in our front yard come Monday morning, bright and early. Now I figured them hogs were probably multiplying every day that I delayed. I probably wasn't far off either; those things in the wild are prolific little buggers.

Sure enough, before daylight Monday morning, the hounds set up an awful racket as I stepped out onto the porch. My eyes I reckon, dang near leaped outta my head. It had to be my hog man; I could smell him from where I stood. Two of the boniest horses I had ever seen stood hip shot at the gate and in the wagon were at least six of the ugliest dogs ever created. All teeth and jaws with lots of scars lining their sides, and dang near bony as the horses.

The old man sitting atop the wagon seat, was I reckon, about as skinny as the rest of the outfit. However, he had the brightest pair of blue eyes I have ever seen. They were alive in that old withered, suntanned face and they seemed to sparkle when he focused in on you. No sir, this old man didn't look like much, but as the man said, looks can be very deceiving.

Pa walked out to the wagon with me following him as close as I could get. The nearer to that wagon we got, the worse the smell became. Now it was almost breakfast time that meant it was only good manners to invite the stranger in to eat. I was wondering when that aroma hit the kitchen, who was gonna be in the most trouble, me or Pa. I mean he done the inviting. It wasn't that Granny wasn't hospitable, but that smell, whew, it was enough to stop a skunk smooth dead in its tracks, poor Granny believed that cleanliness was next to Godliness.

I watched intently as that old man slowly unraveled himself and climbed down from that rickety old wagon. How in the world was this scarecrow of what use to be a man, moving slowly as a ten legged snail, gonna catch the fastest things on four feet in these parts. I don't mind telling you, it was starting to make me have some concerns. Was old Jess having some fun with me? Behind me, I could hear RC and Joann snickering from the porch.

Right about then the old man told Pa who he was and asked if he be me. When Pa pointed at me, the skinny man looked down his long pencil nose and those blue eyes twinkled. I reckon he didn't think any more of me than I did of him. Finally he stuck out a grimy paw and rung my hand like he was shaking with another man. Introducing himself as Phineus Pallito Phillabaum from Abilene, Texas then he finally released my hand. He'd been over at Ardmore catching a few wild hogs when Jess had sent him the letter. I shook my head slowly; Jess had made the deal with Phineus before I had agreed on anything. Yep Old Jess knew I was in trouble for sure.

Well when we started through the door for breakfast Joann and RC stopped their snickering and grabbed for their noses. I mean to tell you that Mister Phineus was ripe for sure. That was the quietest bunch around the table that morning you ever didn't hear. I guess they were afraid to speak and open their mouth for fear of the stink getting in.

Anyway, we all survived breakfast, matter of fact, by the time Pa had his third cup of coffee, I was beginning to feel better about Phineus. From the stories he told, he'd been to someplace called Russia and had learned all about hog catching and such. By now, I was starting to see money in my pocket. I don't know how good a hog man he was, but at least he talked a good story and that was a whole lot better than anybody else around here was doing. We couldn't even see hogs much less get them suckers in a pen.

Old Phineus said he planned on starting first thing in the morning after he'd set up camp and kinda learnt the lay of the land and such. He didn't need to learn about our farm cause if he did get on somebody else's land they'd welcome him with open arms. The hogs had done wore out their welcome hereabouts. What them ornery things hadn't rooted up, they completely destroyed. Crops, gardens, riverbanks, and the people themselves had been the victims of a mule-footed hog at least once.

Well as the old saying goes, I was there with bells on the next morning, as I wasn't about to miss out on the start of this show, no siree bob. Now Phineus had all his hounds chained up except one middle size white dog that sure 'nuff weren't a hound. I'd never seen anything quite like him before. Phineus told me he was a terrier of some kind and he was the Judas goat he used for hog catching. I reckon that went over my head, as I didn't rightly know what a Judas goat was, but I was willing to learn. Man, I was willing to listen or to try anything. Like the man said, I was in deep do do.

The old hog man asked me where we would most likely jump a hog. I looked at him kinda funny I guess, because he shrugged his shoulders. I just waved my hand, it didn't matter, they'd liable to be most anywhere. I watched curiously, as he strapped some leather leggings around the horse's legs reaching clear past their knees. Next, we hooked the team up to the smaller wagon with the high sideboards.

Phineus pronounced we were ready to engage the enemy, I thought we were gonna catch them not fight'em. He always talked funny like that; I guess he did have some book learning. Turning loose two of his skinniest hounds, I figured they were redbones; he left the rest trailing on ropes behind the wagon. The smaller white dog rode beside us on the seat. I guess he had special status because all the while he was here, he never walked anywhere. I figured that was because he was a Judas dog or whatever Phineus called him.

The red dogs hadn't been gone five minutes when both of them opened up. They had themselves a trail and it was hot. Phineus left that wagon faster than a greased pig and turned the rest of his hounds loose. I didn't figure he could move that fast. What a race, man those dogs were laying the law down on that track. The white dog whined a little but he didn't make a move to leave the wagon. I figured Phineus would tear out on the track, but to my consternation, he just let them horses walk along slow like. They seemed to know the game as they were following that pack of hounds.

It was a race for sure and then all of a sudden things went to happening. The horses picked up their pace into a slow trot and Phineus and that white dog had their eyes to the wind. I swear they looked like two bird dogs pointing with their noses. We found the dogs bayed up in a small back water slough than ran down to the river. Them dogs had about twenty hogs surrounded and were giving them lots of lip service.

Every now and then, a hog would charge but the dogs would first retreat then push them back into the group. I had to hand it to the dogs, they were tough. Phineus had a couple hounds he called Airedales that would flat take a hog to the ground. He said they were half bulldog, whatever they were; they were rough in a fight.

Quickly, we got the wagon in position and let down the tailgate. Phineus told me I best stay on the wagon seat, which suited me, just fine. He got a good grip on the rope that raised and lowered the tailgate of the smaller wagon then whistled at the white dog. Now I'm telling you folks, I've seen a few shows, but that little dog takes the cake. He got out there between them hogs and the wagon and started barking and rolling around on the ground. The other dogs backed out leaving him all alone. I thought he was having a fit, sure looked like it to me.

Quick as a frog's blink those hogs charged that dog and followed him right up into that wagon. Every time they'd sull up and not move, the white dog would get close to them and start rolling all over the ground and growling. Sure enough, those hogs would charge again and first thing you know, we had eight good-sized hogs in that wagon bed. Old Phineus whooped and slammed the gate shut.

I didn't know where that dog was going cause that wagon bed wasn't near big enough for the hogs and him too. Just as I thought they had him for sure out there, he came right through a small hole that was made in the front of the wagon. Next thing you know Phineus crowded them hogs further up front and petitioned them off and we were off after another bunch.

By dark, I was tired but we already captured twenty-five hogs and I was mighty proud of Phineus and his hounds. Pa and RC came down to look at our captives and stayed to listen to the story. They had heard the hounds running all day and even heard some of the fighting. There had been a lot of that, one of the dogs was cut bad and out of action for awhile. Old Phineus stitched him up quicker than a doctor could and it looked like pretty good sewing to me.

Phineus was right, that white dog was worth his weight in gold, he was a Judas dog. With the other hounds surrounding the hogs, that white dog would tease them into following him right up into that wagon. What a show, I went to bed that night dreaming of becoming a hog man myself. Providing of course, I didn't have to smell as bad as Phineus. Granny wasn't so keen on the idea of me going off hog hunting with old Phineus but RC seemed to think it a fine idea. He figured it might be a good way to be rid of me.

The next day RC came along to watch the fun. It was almost a repeat of the day before and we got another dog cut up. Them old boars with their long tusks were bad to the bone and they were gritty as could be. I was wondering if we'd have enough dogs left to catch the other hogs but Phineus said not to worry.

The third day we left off our hog catching and laid around camp. I had to admit old Phineus wasn't ate up with energy, kinda reminded me a lot of me. Along about dinner Roy Dobbs showed up with his big truck and we started loading pigs into it. I never did know how Mister Dobbs knew when to show up but I was glad he did. We already had all the hogs them wagons would hold and I was eager to get back to hunting.

I finally figured out what the leather leggings were on the horses for when I saw several hogs charge past the dogs and made Phineus clamor to safety atop the wagon. Them hogs slashed at the horse's legs as they ran under them. Any one of our horses would have had himself a fit and pitched a rodeo if a hog grabbed onto their legs. Not these, they just stood there as calm as if nothing was happening until the dogs ran them back into a group. The rawhide leggings were cut up some and they saved the horses legs from injury.

As the days passed, I stayed with Phineus and directed him where to move his wagon to, but day by day the races became fewer and the catch for the day tallied less. I kept a running figure notched on a small limb every day. As of today, I sat and counted one hundred twenty six notches. I didn't figure there to be many more hogs left running loose.

Tom Caldwell from Milburn sent RC to inform Phineus of a bunch of hogs over on him, about four miles west of where we were camped. I had set around our campfire listening to the old hog hunter spin his tales of countries and people he met on his hog hunting adventures. It was almost like being in school, only a lot more interesting.

I could tell RC didn't believe some of Phineus' tales the way he rolled his eyes, but he didn't say so. Why I'll bet Phineus could have taught our schoolteacher a few things if he had put his mind to it. You know Phineus lost the bad smell he had when I first met him. I figured he had taken himself a bath or something.

We gathered up and moved on downriver where we gathered

another twenty-five hogs then after two more days of nothing, Phineus decided we caught them all. Phineus had one last dinner with us before pulling out. I still remember him waving that old black hat of his as he rounded the bend. I never did see him again, but I've still got the Remington Twenty-Two he gave me for my part of the hogs. Oh yea, I forgot, I think I've still got some of the scratches Granny put on me as she tried to scrub the hog smell from me with that dang horse brush and lye soap. I tried to tell her I didn't smell a thing.

After that Pa told us to shoot every hog we seen running loose in the bottoms, but I never did. Phineus cleaned them out pretty good and when I did see one, it reminded me of the old hog hunter, all I could do was grin and watch the pig waddle away. Anyhoo that was the end of my hog ranching days. I wouldn't say I was a failure at my first business venture, but I was sure happy to be rid of them ornery little rascals. With all that had happened, I felt I was getting old as the hot days of summer passed, shucks at this rate I'd be shaving before too much longer, maybe ten or twelve years.

Chapter 13
Palomino Horse

It was deep summer again and man, it was hot. Besides going to school, we didn't do much but lay in the shade or go swimming. Back in them days, every good shade tree had itself one or two iron beds conveniently located under its cool branches. Unless it was chore time or we had to bust the middles out of our garden patch, we'd be laid up under the shade or on the river like a bunch of dead drift logs. No sir, we weren't about to waste energy until we just sure 'nuff had to. Even Pa didn't move about much except for our chores until sundown brought us a little reprieve from the heat. I listened as the old-timers talked about the heat and how they hadn't seen it this hot since the early thirties. I swear it was so hot, even the little horned toads were sweating.

Walking through the cornfields you could almost hear the corn hollering. "Water, water." Now I know for a fact that corn don't talk, but then again? To tell the truth, back in them days I weren't none too energetic, but with the heat and all you might say I was downright lazy. Course now, I weren't alone, everything on the place seemed to be laid up in the shade, from the hounds to the chickens.

It was so hot in the schoolhouse, Mister Rowland would let us kids stay outside and study under the huge oak trees that dotted the schoolyard. Even the marble shooting and fist fighting slowed down to a snail's pace. If a fight did take place, it was a mighty serious matter. Right about the hottest time of the day, we were all about to wilt like a blade of new cut grass when this brand spanking new automobile pulls up right next to our merry-go-round. What pops out of that car was the fattest woman I ever did see and right behind her is none other than Thaddeus Archibald Baldwin.

No, I ain't putting you on, that was his handle, all of it. I ain't joshing you, old Thaddeus had on short pants and suspenders and real shoes. On top of that, he had on some kind of thing around his neck. He later said it was a bow tie, which he confessed he hated. His mother insisted he wear it as they were rich folks and she wanted him to look sophisticated and all. He wasn't about to cross her, which in that I don't blame him one little bit. Why if that big woman landed on you in a fit, she could do some serious damage to your body.

Thaddeus stood there beside his mother; leastways he was in the shade, as Mister Rowland walked over and introduced himself to her. I was kinda intrigued to say the least as the feller in the front seat, who I thought was the father, never moved a muscle. Later on we found out he was the chauffeur, that's the man who drove their car. I reckon Mrs. Baldwin never learned how to drive, shucks I didn't know how myself. Course now, I could at least get behind that little old wheel that steered the automobile but I doubt Mrs. Baldwin could.

Thaddeus' father himself turned out to be our new banker up in Durant and they purchased the old Sawyer place up the road. After Mrs. Baldwin assured Thaddeus she'd be back to pick him up when school let out, her and the chauffeur roared down the road in a cloud of dust. They left the poor thing standing there all alone like one of them Jewish people in a den of lions. Leastways I figured that's the way he felt, shucks if it had been me I would have felt that way. Us Okies aren't the friendliest looking bunch of folks. Now, I had to hand it to him, he didn't seem scared.

I kinda felt sorry for him you might say, so I wandered out in the heat and stuck out my hand like I seen the men do and introduced myself. I knew what the other kids were thinking; the dang fool didn't have enough sense to come in out of the sun. Old Thaddeus was something, I swear he had on big old black rimmed glasses and the glass in them things was so thick it made his eyes twice their normal size. You know he was downright likable, that is, when you got past the funny looking part of him. He had the skinniest legs I ever seen on anything and great big knees. Not only that, he was as pigeon toed as a cross-eyed duck, which made him waddle kinda the same way.

The boy had that natural smile that made you take to him like a newborn puppy. I propelled him over to the shade and motioned for him to sit. As he was about to plop down under a tree, an acorn the size of a small hen egg hit him right square in the bottom of those pretty short pants. Glancing over at the other boys, I knew right off it was Delmar Perkins that had let go with the acorn. You see Delmar was kinda the schoolyard bully and he enjoyed his job. Me and him went at it tooth and claw on several occasions. Most of the time I wound up on the losing end, till finally I guess he got tired of pounding on me and left me alone. Now he had a new victim to abuse.

Thaddeus never flinched or said a thing; he just set there talking to me like nothing happened. I know that acorn had to of hurt, because I had been on the receiving end of them things many a time. Normally I would have thought him a coward or something like that. For some reason when he winked at me and went on talking, I started taking a second look at my new friend.

Kinda like a new mule or horse, when you get to looking closer, things start to look different. Yea old Thaddeus was skinny alright, with bony old knuckles and long lean muscled up arms. Not the bunched up kind the girls like, no these muscles were like cords running under his skin. But it was the eyes that took my interest, they showed no emotion, even when Delmar sauntered over with the other boys, real cocky like, and pulled off that bow tie thing from Thaddeus' shirt.

Delmar clipped it on his own shirt and walked away laughing and still Thaddeus didn't move or say anything. Right then and there, I got me a suspicion that old Delmar was about to get himself into a hornet's nest. Now I wasn't sure you know, but have you ever seen an old water moccasin laying in the trail just watching you, if you have then you know what I'm talking about. About then Mister Rowland hollered for class to commence once again and we all hated it, as we trooped back inside that hot schoolroom.

Sure enough at the end of the school day Mrs. Baldwin and her car was Johnny on the spot. I was kinda hoping she'd be running a might late. Delmar had been making faces and was working himself up to pounce on Thaddeus, and I for one wanted to see the wreck. With mine and his history, I was a hoping it was old Delmar that got himself wrecked. I was really beginning to take a liking to Thaddeus and decided to take up for him against Delmar. Well, I mentioned the fact to him but when he cut them cold blue eyes at me I decided I'd let him do his own fighting.

The next morning was Thursday and Thaddeus was again delivered to school and wouldn't you know it, he had on another one of them bow tie things. Come dinnertime, we were all sitting out under the shade again. Here comes Delmar and his cronies and quicker than a catfish can swallow a hook, he grabbed Thaddeus' bow tie and walked off. Nothing, I mean Thaddeus didn't move, protest, or even run to Mister Rowland. I was getting curious about the boy to say the least. Maybe I had been wrong maybe he was scared.

Now I've been wrong once or twice in my short life and this time I was definitely wrong. He wasn't scared, the boy was smart like a fox. See the way he explained it after old Delmar departed was, he had three of them things his Mama made him wear. He hated'em, every one of them, so if things worked out just right old Delmar would have complete possession of the bow ties by Friday. Course now Mrs. Baldwin could come to school and land square in the middle of Delmar with all her, ah, let's say size, now that would be something to see too. If she lit on him, poor Delmar would be flattened like a pancake.

It worked out just perfect, by Friday Delmar had all three bow ties and Thaddeus was grinning from ear to ear. It would take at least a month for his Mama to send off for more in the Sears and Roebucks wish catalog, yep just perfect. Still, old Delmar was itching to fight, taking the bow ties hadn't worked, so all the following week he aggravated Thaddeus worse than two crows on a hoot owl. Thaddeus said nothing, just sat there and smiled. He did ask me which way Delmar lived and like a fool, I told him.

The next day his Mama wasn't driving the car, nope it was just Thaddeus and the chauffeur, Shamiro Shihito, or something like that. Funny looking little feller, not real tall, he had dark black hair, yellowish skin, and real slanty eyes. Delmar had been up to his bullying all day, calling out names and whizzing an acorn our way ever now and then. Old Thaddeus took it all in stride, just squatting there like an old sitting hen. Now, Mister Rowland wasn't aware of anything going on, no, Thaddeus wasn't a tattletale, not by a long shot.

Anyway, dat burnit I missed it, that car sat in the shade of an oak tree until all of us kids were far from the school. I seen it head back towards Milburn, not towards Thaddeus' place. I thought something was funny but wasn't for sure until the next morning. Poor old Delmar looked like he'd been trampled by a herd of Jackson's bulls, then ate up and spit out by the hogs. The Fox boys had seen it though, what little there was of it to see and they told it, blow by blow.

They had been walking home with Delmar when the Baldwin car passed and let Thaddeus out. What a wreck, they were still shaking their heads in wonderment. They said Thaddeus never said a word as he walked up and decked old Delmar, knocking him head first into the dirt road. Then apparently, from what they said it all went downhill from there on as those bony knuckles were landing flush on Delmar's ugly face faster than a flustered hornet. They said they never seen anyone fight the way Thaddeus had, but he got the job done, good and proper. Jimmy Fox told how Thaddeus flipped poor old Delmar every which way but loose then chopped him somehow with the side of his hand. To top off the day, Thaddeus had asked the Fox boys if they wanted to try their luck, they said he even told them he would take both of them on at the same time. They owned up to it, they were Delmar's buddies alright but this time they told me Delmar was on his own. There was no way they was gonna fight old Thaddeus.

I had to miss it, the fight of the year and I was walking the wrong way. I'd have walked clean to Milburn to have seen it, drats. Poor old Delmar looked like a black man the next day. Poor thing had knots and welts all over his ugly little face, but you know I think it broke him from sucking eggs, bullying I mean. Yes Sir, he was downright peaceful for the rest of the year.

Was kinda funny though, the next day Delmar's Pappy was at school I reckon to settle the score. Seems Delmar described Thaddeus as quite a bit older and several pounds bigger than he was. You should have seen Mister Perkins' face, that's Delmar's pappy when he got a good gander at Thaddeus wearing one of his new bow ties. I swear his face turned purple, then he looked down at Delmar and clenched his fists several times before he got back in his wagon and drove off. One thing was certain the next day, Delmar must have gotten the strapping of his life because he sure didn't sit down all day or the next either.

Me and Thaddeus became the best of friends until his Pappy moved to Tulsa, yes sir we were good friends. I sure would have liked to have seen that fight though.

It was the hottest summer I could ever remember, not that I'm that old but it was sure hot. We were all walking up the lane to the house when we spied Pa leading a yeller horse ahead of us. Roy Dobbs must have dropped him off on the main road, as he was only a few yards ahead. That old horse was a looker for sure but I was a wondering what Pa wanted him for. Palomino in color, with a white mane and tail, he carried himself with his neck arched and a prance in his step. He was pretty, but Pa always said pretty didn't get the job done. Around the farm if you didn't work to a harness, you weren't staying long.

We all started watching closer as Pa led the horse and not paying any attention to the animal. Every few feet, that Palomino would reach out and strike with a front foot at Pa's turned back. I was a thinking to myself, horse you hit him and you ain't gonna like the outcome of what happens next. We followed along behind, me, RC, and Joann and every few feet he'd strike out then kinda bounce on his rear end.

Pa had put him in the mule lot when we reached the yard. Now me, being a horse lover deluxe, raced over to the pen and climbed onto the top rail. I was already having elusions of me riding that yeller horse down the main street of Milburn. Squatting there like a treed squirrel admiring the animal I looked off for only a second when next thing I know Pa's a hollering for me to get down. When I looked up that beast was a charging the fence I was on, his teeth bared, his ears laid back, and he was coming fast. I vacated the premises you might say and in a hurry. That horse shouldered into that fence so hard it rattled and shook for ten minutes. Then that ornery cuss stood across the fence looking between the poles at me and pawing the ground.

I've been around horses all my life and I never had seen one charge a man like this one just done. Me and him was gonna have to come to an understanding and quick. I watched Pa disappear inside the house shaking his head and pointing his finger at me. Quick as a blink, out of my pocket comes my slingshot. When that rock hit him in the rump old yeller retreated to the other side of the lot, his ears laid back and shaking his head.

Positioning myself back on the top rail, I sat there daring that horse to come at me again. One thing was for certain, he weren't a total idiot and he never made one move towards me again. Pa hollered for me to get down and start on my chores. I did, but not before sticking my tongue out at yeller and then I slowly climbed back down to the ground.

Well every night when RC got in from school him and Pa would work with old yeller for a spell before chore time. That horse wasn't an idiot nope he was plumb outlaw. He took the studs and wouldn't lead, matter of fact he wouldn't do nothing, just balk. Pa hissed Rover onto him and after a couple bites to his heels, he decided it'd be easier if he just came along. Next, they saddled him up then tied him behind the wagon. That sucker took the studs again and dang near pulled that wagon into two pieces when he set back on the lead rope.

Pa looped the rope around his girth, ran it back through the rope halter, and clucked to the team. Man what a wreck, when that rope tightened up so did old yeller. I never seen so much rearing and plunging, and bucking at any rodeo I ever been to. The rear end of that wagon was jumping around like a dat burn cricket, but Pa just kept the horses pulling old yeller around and around the stomp lot. Finally, Rover was called in again to set the old horse straight and put a little go into him.

Finally he leveled out and started following meek as a lamb, not that I ever seen any lambs, but that's what I've heard. I got to hand it to RC, he volunteered to climb on that idgit, but Pa said no. Me, I had already given up on any thoughts of riding Yeller into Milburn. RC said he'd ride him again, but Pa refused, I knew he was tempted. No, this old horse was dangerous, he'd rear up and fall backwards quicker than Granny could flip a pancake. Probably squash you like a bug if he caught you in the middle between the saddle horn and the ground.

Pa filled up a couple tow sacks about half full of sand, tied them together, and then eased them over old yeller's back. Nothing that yeller horse stood there real quiet, his eyes closed like he was almost asleep. Well Pa climbed back onto the wagon seat and clucked to the team, let me tell you when that lead rope tightened you talk about a wreck, my eyes were bigger that saucers. Old yeller sat back and I mean that team was plowing furrows with all four of his feet. We could have planted ourselves a row of corn right there. Next thing I know old yeller lunged straight forward and got in that poor little old wagon, how I don't know, but he did.

He was laying kinda sideways, upside down, kicking and bawling, matter of fact he kicked the side boards clean off the wagon bed. Well Pa up and decided it was time for him to depart the wagon which he done, and in record time. The team ran into a corner of the lot and squatted there, their eyes bigger than mine. Old yeller up and flung himself out of the wagon, hitting the ground, and went to bawling and bucking like a big old beached catfish, nearly jerking his own dang fool head off. Finally, that poor old cotton rope broke and yeller went head over heels backwards.

Believe it or not, when he finally got to his feet he still had them sandbags across the saddle and he was tearing up the ground. Right about then Rover couldn't stand it any longer. He ties into Old Yeller and we had us a show for sure. That old horse was bucking and kicking, the sandbags were banging his sides with every jump, and Rover would grab him a mouthful of horse hock at every opportunity. Man, what a show, I think right about then RC decided he weren't no bronc rider after all, leastways I never heard him offer to ride that yeller horse again.

Well next thing you know that old horse plowed through the yard fence and had his head stuck up against the side of the house just a jumping up and down. He was sure 'nuff making that old house rock. Granny and everyone else ran outside thinking there was a cyclone in among us for sure. Man, if I hadn't of been so shocked I would have laughed myself silly.

That horse was all lathered up and a sweating, with his old sides heaving in and out like a bellows when Pa finally managed to get hold of what was left of the rope. I don't think Pa was so worried about that horse as he was about his saddle. It was the only one we had and it weren't much but least it was rideable. Us kids always rode bareback but Pa, he needed a saddle for sure.

Anyway, that was old Yeller's last chance you might say. I think Pa had notions of just shooting the idiot but he shipped him out with Roy the next week to the soap factory. Somebody somewhere is probably washing their hands with him. I wished Dad would have been home at the time, he was a bronc rider, and that would have been a show for sure. I still daydream about riding that horse down the main street of Milburn, he was a beauty. Only thing wrong with that dream was the way it ended. Seems in my dream that old yeller horse threw me as I was passing Mary Peaster's house. When I came to, she was holding my head in her lap and all the town kids were laughing their heads off. What a nightmare, I didn't sleep for a week after that.

Chapter 14
The Long Race

Halloween was on us and the nights were already starting to get a little frosty. Our crops were in and most of our firewood was hauled up to the huge woodpile so we were sitting comfortable as far as work went. The fields were laid by for next spring's planting and the garden wasn't beckoning to us. Except for our regular chores around the farm, we were on our own.

It had been a good year, Pa was happy and when he was in a good mood, everybody was. Shucks, I was even making pretty good grades in school. Now Joann was the brains of the outfit, it was almost disgusting her being so smart and all, but I guess we were all proud of her. Me, I thought I was doing good to get a "C" along with my "D's" most of the time. Now, it wasn't that I was dumb; it was just that the woods and the outdoors beckoned to me when I was sitting in that old schoolhouse. I couldn't help it, daydreaming just came natural to me I reckon. So did Mister Rowland's paddle, I got more than my fair share, I'll say one thing though, I earned every one of them licks I received.

We didn't know it yet, but this was Thaddeus' last year with us. He and his family were moving up to the big time, the big city. Just when we got him straightened out, his clothes and all. He had bucked his mother on the short pants issue and after getting himself a good thumping, she finally let him have his way. If only we could do something about those glasses but he was as blind as a crossed-eyed billy goat without them. I always wondered how he could see to fight with no glasses, but he could.

I invited him to spend the weekend with us cause I knew we'd be heading to town Saturday morning bright and early and I wanted to see Thaddeus wreck them town boys. I didn't let on about it, but I knew them smart aleck locals would be on me the minute they caught wind we were in town. Me and Thaddeus were good friends, so I figured he'd help out in a tight. I had finally found out the strange little man that worked for Mister Baldwin was Japanese and he had taught Thaddeus all about some strange kind of fighting. It might have been strange, but it worked. Old Delmar would testify to that, after that last little go round you couldn't melt and pour the boy on Thaddeus. Well, I missed that one but I sure was gonna pay attention today in town.

I had set Thaddeus up to a Coca-Cola Soda Pop and a Baby Ruth Candy Bar figuring he'd need his strength. I didn't intentionally start a fight but somehow word had spread around town that I was gonna be out back of the old gymnasium soon as we'd finished our refreshments. My eyes were already watering, nope wasn't from the bite them little old cokes used to have, no sir, it was pure anticipation, that's what it were.

Sure enough, those uppity city kids were Johnny on the spot. Soon as we arrived, they started gathering like they were going to the show or something. Poor old Thaddeus didn't have any idea what was fixing to take place but as soon as the kids started making fun of his glasses, he figured it out. When Thaddeus flipped that first kid, almost wrenching his arm from its socket, I motioned to the leader of the town brats to have a seat in the shade and we'd go at it after the show was over. Man it was like butter over hot cakes, smooth, Thaddeus went through them kids like corn through a duck, what a show. I wouldn't have missed it for a hundred cat eye marbles.

Anyway, the black eye and bloody nose that I took home with me that day were worth the trouble. Thaddeus said he would give me some pointers as my fighting ability needed improvement, but hunting always came first, we just never seemed to find the time, then he was gone. With my loose mouth, I sure could have used at least a few of his lessons, funny thing I never looked for a fight but they sure looked for me.

I recall the last time me and him went hunting with RC and the Dunn's boys. It were a prime night, no wind, quiet as a church house. We were all standing down at the river crossing listening to the night sounds and the water rippling across the exposed rocks. RC looked up at the full moon that seemed to shimmer off the river and shook his head. That was the only thing messing the night up. If those hounds struck a boar coon what we called a ridge runner in this light, he'd lead'em on a merry chase. I never figured out why, but on a moonlight night an old smart coon is almost impossible to get up a tree.

There's just something about standing there in the dark of the night; the sounds, the quiet, and it's so peaceful. In addition, you're waiting in anticipation to hear the long opening bawl of the hounds striking old ringtail's trail and the excitement of the other dogs joining in the race. Man I loved it, nothing equaled the thrill of the chase. Those tall trees along the riverbank sometimes seemed to beckon me, almost like eerie ghosts standing silently with their long arms extending down to the river. I knew the shape of most every one of them but the darkness cast a completely different light on everything. The glow of the moon glimmering across the quiet river, man what a great feeling. Standing there in the company of your friends, alone with your thoughts, we wait on the hounds to open and the race to start. A lone whippoorwill sounding off somewhere in the dark and further down river an old horned owl let loose, his deep bass call booming along the water.

From out of the dark came the cry as Fanny struck first, her sharp bawl beckoning us to follow unaware of what was in store for us this night. I'll tell you this much, it was the dangdest race I ever heard of, one I'll never forget. After it was over, I was thankful Pa hadn't been with us, it might have been too much for his ticker. He was like them dogs, he wasn't about to quit a great race like this one turned out to be. I swear them dogs were a bawling and carrying on like they were looking that old coon right in the eye every minute of the race. We had three of our old dogs in the race, Rover, Quane, Fanny, and the Dunn's brought along one of their Bluetick pups. Rover looked him over right smart but went on down the river. He hadn't forgotten the other Blueticks and his grudge against them but as this was just a pup, he didn't set on him.

That old coon headed due east in high gear cause them dogs were flat toting the mail and closing in on him at every jump. We listened awhile as we lit our carbide lights then crossed the river and started on their trail, our ears following the sound of the race far ahead. Now nobody owned a watch back then or for that matter would have carried one if they had. It seemed like them hounds had been running for at least an hour. RC only shook his head as we plodded on. He hadn't forgotten the bobcat incident; it was definitely still fresh in his mind. Tim didn't speak of it either but I bet that old cat was still fresh on his mind too. This time I figured it was probably an old boar and one of them ridge runners that occasionally we'd strike. Those dogs were a running fast and hard. There was no way they were gonna lose this coon. A smart old ringtail can be a slippery little rascal and we just hoped that's what we were in hot pursuit of.

RC had cut across leading us due west hoping our quarry would circle back and sure enough we weren't far off when Rover finally gave his tree bark. The dogs slowly made a big loop back to the river. They were looking up a large oak tree barking their heads off. From all the growling and baying going on we all thought they had caught Mister Coon on the ground but that wasn't the case at all. Shining our lights at the base of that old oak almost at the river's edge, we saw that coon and he was a big'un. That sucker had somehow gotten himself under the tree and wedged in behind the roots where the dirt had washed away during the floods and high water times. We just thought the dogs were looking up; actually they were looking straight into the face of that coon.

I swear he looked like he was in a jail cell, not that I had ever seen one myself. There was no way the hounds could get to him and he seemed to know it. That coon was just sitting there looking out at all of us calm as a sulled possum. One thing was for sure, we had him, or did we? He couldn't get out; trouble was the dogs couldn't get in.

We had four dogs around the base of that tree and there was five of us, we had all avenues of escape covered, yes sir, it was foolproof we had him, but I'll be danged. One minute we were all gathered around prodding that coon trying to figure how to get him out of that jail. The next thing we know, he pulled a Houdini on us and vanished out the back door. I strained my eyes trying to locate that sucker; I just knew he couldn't have given us all the slip. Finally, I gave up looking and conceding our furry friend had vanished. I looked down the banks as far as I could with the carbide and there he was, waddling up river like he had all the time in the world. I swear that coon was a looking back grinning at us and we stood there open mouthed looking back at him. For once Rover and Quane had been fooled. They were still digging at the base of the tree never realizing their opponent had done broke jail or as they said back then made his getaway.

I latched on to the nearest hound and drug him to the trail, trouble was when I turned him loose that fool pup ran right back to the tree. Finally we got Rover on the trail and the race was on again. About a half mile farther up river the banks became real steep. We heard a fight going on, them hounds had caught mister coon in the water. Running to get there on time before one of them dogs up and got himself drowned we spotted the coon climbing up a dead limb hanging in the water.

Those hounds were beside themselves trying to climb that sandy bank. Finally RC managed to call them off and get them on top and back on the trail. We hadn't gone hardly anywhere when lo and behold ahead of us was a foot log across the river and guess what set atop it? Our quarry, that's what. That coon was sitting there like he had just sat down to the supper table and calmly looking down at the dogs.

I swear, now I've been known to stretch the truth a time or two, but I ain't this time, no sir, don't have to. That coon was licking the water from himself and seemed to be grinning again. Next thing I knew Rover was on the foot log and the race was on again. Now I know all of this had been going on at least two hours all told and we still didn't have the coon. Next time we'd have him. We better because I was getting pretty tired. Sure enough, up river they trailed just a bawling and telling us all about it. Directly they turned due west again and recrossed the river, at least they were headed for home.

We all thought the coon was headed for his home den, later we found out different. Next thing I know the dogs treed again, we had him for sure this time. When we got to where they were we all blinked, all the dogs were treeing alright, but there was not a tree in sight, just flat ground on the bank of the river. That flat ground was bare as a hungry hounds plate, nothing, just dirt. Rover started digging into the ground as we stood and scratched our heads. RC laid himself down and looked over the bank. Sure enough there was a hole in the sandy bank about two feet down on the steep sandy bank.

Dragging some leaves and twigs into the hole RC lowered me and the pup and gave instructions for me to light the fire. Well it wouldn't burn good, but it sure was smoking the place up and that was the idea, just hot enough to force the coon out. All of a sudden smoke started coming out from above where Rover was digging at the bare ground. Now there sat me and that Bluetick pup perched with a death hold on the side of that cut bank, which was steep and slick, trying to blink out the smoke that was boiling back in our face and eyes. The pup wanted to vacate the premises and get back on top where the other dogs were barking and carrying on but I had me a good death grip on his collar.

Tim Dunn hollered when he seen the smoke from Rover's hole in the ground and that stupid pup lunged about the same time thinking like me that they had the coon. I had my hands full for sure, holding onto a dead root with one hand and the pup with the other, dangling on the side of that steep bank. The next thing I knew between blinks I had me about thirty pounds of mad coon running smooth flat over my scrawny little body. The fact was that sucker wasn't one bit happy. I tried my best to kick him back but all that accomplished was he up and took a bite of my boot, latched onto the sole he did, so I commenced to kick harder to get him loose from me. I wasn't about to yell for help, I wanted to sure enough, would have to; trouble was, I had my hands full and didn't have time to yell. That thing looked as big as me, and he was a lot madder.

Thank goodness that coon was more intent on escaping the fire, which singed his hair some, than eating me alive. I might have let out a cussword; I ain't sure, that blasted coon, me, and that stupid dog, all landed in the river ten feet down. Now we ain't talking summertime and we definitely ain't talking about wading water. I was about to get myself drowned dead and I didn't have any idea where that crazy coon was. Coughing up water I reached out and latched on to the Bluetick who had spotted the coon and swam by in hot pursuit. I hung on for dear life, there was no way I could swim out of there by myself with a heavy coat and shoes plumb full of river water.

Luckily the dog headed for the nearest bank and he slowly drug me to shallow water. I don't think RC even knew what had happened to me as they were still on top hollering. I let go the pup and he went after the coon bawling and squalling. I was soaked to the gills, wringing out my clothes when the rest finally found a place to cross, and walked back to where I sat. My teeth were chattering like a magpie and I definitely was not in a good mood. Shoot, I could have been mauled to death, drowned, catch pneumonia, and all they wanted to do was build me a fire then leave me here while they hurried to catch up to the dogs.

I didn't need me any fire and I sure wasn't staying behind and missing the fun. Slipping back on my wet boots I informed them I was ready and away we went. That coon had done dealt me some misery, now it was his turn. That is providing we ever caught him. Thaddeus was dry so he insisted I wear his coat, which I truly was thankful for.

The race was on again, the hounds were way out front and running hard. In all my days of coon hunting I ain't never seen a coon run this far and this long. We treed him three times already and he got the best of us each time. Well we were determined, I admired him and all that stuff but it was now a matter of honor. He had done up and made a fool of us all night, now he was gonna pay, I hoped. Not to mention the fact that I was wet, cold, and miserable. I was almost mad enough to fight that coon myself if the dogs ever treed him. Well almost, you ever seen a mad coon coming at you all teeth and hair, on second thought I guess I wasn't all that mad.

I heard Quane hit a tree and I grinned, hot dog, we had him this time. That old redbone didn't bark up a tree unless she had the hair in the tree. Wrong, we got to the tree just about the same time Rover quit the tree and went to trailing again. RC was baffled but it didn't take long to figure how the coon had given them the slip this time. The old pecan had a broken limb that crossed to another tree and that's where he went, across that limb then down to the ground and off a running.

That made four times now we treed him and we still were running. I was cold, wet, and now I had blisters on my heels from running in wet boots. I was determined that coon wasn't gonna make me quit the race. There was no way this coon was about to give us the slip, not with Rover out in the front and running hot. I had faith in that red dog. No sir, I knew we had him this time; he was headed straight away from the river across flat pastureland.

We were heading due north when all of a sudden them dogs shut up. We all pulled to a stop and waited for a tree bark, nothing, them hounds were quieter than a cemetery on Sunday. Starting forward towards where we had last heard them, we listened, hoping for any kind of bark. Well we had our answer quick enough. A quarter mile further on we smelled it, a burn. Frank Waddell had been burning off some dead grass and down timber and our fast thinking coon managed to run right through the middle of it. Now even a wonder dog like Rover, plus Quane's great nose couldn't smell him in the still smoking ashes.

I stood there soaking wet looking at the rest, and then we all started to laugh. No we hadn't got that old ringtail but we experienced the race of our lives, a race that none of us was ever likely to forget. That was the last coon hunt me and Thaddeus ever went on. You should always save the best for last. For once and once only, old Rover met his match that night. I smiled then nodded off into the dark, knowing there would always be another race. Well fact is, that old ringtail deserved to get away; he outsmarted us all night. I wished the old rascal well and hobbled towards home. I heard Mister Rowland say once something about the man that laughs last, laughs longest. I'll bet that old coon is still laughing somewhere down along the banks of Blue River.

Chapter 15
Raft Coon

Hot diggity, fall was here and except for farm chores and the like, all we had to do was go to school and go hunting. Now I could have done without the school, but I sure did like the hunting part. Shucks, I was even willing to do more than my share of the chores if it would get us in the woods quicker. Sunset would come and it turned dark about the same time we finished milking and gobbled down our supper.

Course now Granny always had eggs for us to wash and candle. There were supper dishes to do, which I figured was Joann's job as she didn't help with the milking but as usual, I lost that argument. You know how it is, Joann being the youngest of the kids and a girl, she was spoiled rotten. Now I have to admit, she would turn the handle of the old corn sheller so we could feed the chickens and she would help me shuck the corn. So I wasn't about to let them dirty dishes dampen my spirits, all the time I was sticking my hands into that dishwater I was a figuring on how many we'd tree tonight.

Somehow or another RC always missed out on the girl jobs, but I didn't complain, no sir. Without him, I wouldn't be going hunting as the folks thought me too young to be off by myself. When we were out of hearing RC always said I wouldn't be much of a loss if I didn't come home, you know I never did figure whether he was serious or joking. Funny thing about it, half the time we were running them hounds I was by myself, yep all alone. RC and the Dunn's with their longer legs would up and run off and leave me. I would run off and leave Pa, but somehow we always got to where the dogs were treed, alive and kicking.

Yes sir, all we had to do was go to school, do our chores, and wait for dark. Now Joann she liked school, for the life of me I never knew why. I reckon it was cause she was so much smarter than us simple minded folks. I hated sitting there listening to each kid get up and recite their numbers. I swear I'd wake up sometimes in the middle of the night, reciting like I was in school. Joann was different, I reckon her being a girl and all, she was just more into books and school stuff. I never did see her hardly open a book, and she always made straight A's. I sometimes wondered if she cheated at homework too, like cards. No I knew better, she was just plain smart, something I was never accused of.

No, I never was overly smart but after listening to the older kids recite their lessons for five years I could recite everything the eighth graders could. I'll guarantee you I ain't no brain; back in them days a boy didn't need brains. Girls did, but it don't take a lot of brains to milk a cow, plow a cornfield, or split wood. If you were too smart it could cost you a black eye or two.

Now I got to admit I was fairly smart in some things, as I was always figuring how to get out of work, which normally caused more problems than if I had of just done whatever the work was to begin with. I was a hunter, Daniel Boone and Davy Crockett were my heroes, and by golly they didn't need any education. I always wanted me one of those Coonskin caps they wore, but every time I tried to make one Granny would toss it out the door. I reckon it did smell a little strong for her delicate nose, even the dogs backed away from the hide. The way everybody acted, you'd think it was gonna get up and walk off.

Me, James Rowland, and several of the boys were shooting marbles when the school bell went off; telling us school was fixing to take up. Shucks I was just getting my old shooter working like a top. That marble was a red and white and when it hit solid it would knock a marble out of that ring then set there and spin. No sir, weren't another like it in school, if you lost using it, well, it were your own fault. Sometimes I'd collect five marbles for just letting someone borrow it. Pretty good deal for doing nothing and gambling nothing. It did cost me a black eye or probably several when the guy I loaned it too didn't want to let me have it back. It was worth it, my Pappy always said something worth having is something worth fighting for. I don't figure he was talking about marbles, but that red and white shooter was worth every black eye or bloody nose I received.

Now Almond Rowland, our teacher, was James and Donnie Rowland's daddy and he kept them two young lads a studying hard. He was dead set on them being schoolteachers too. I figured that took a lot of schooling, more than I wanted. Many times as I was listening to the hounds running through the woods, I would think of them two stuck in front of a table and studying their lessons. Well, I weren't planning on being a schoolteacher and putting a bunch of poor kids through misery, no sir, not me.

All the boys were talking about the big coon dog meet that was fixing to take place at Wilson Shico's farm this coming Saturday. It was always a bang up event as coon dogs from all over the county showed up to participate and strut their stuff. Food, dogs, hunting stories, and lots of bragging took up most of the day. I already had half my marbles bet on the outcome of many of the events. I couldn't lose. Shucks, I was on a first name basis with most of the dogs. I knew for a bona fide fact they wouldn't let me down.

I just knew Martin Waddell's dog, Mose, would win the treeing contest hands down. Shucks, that dog could bark faster than Mary Peaster could talk, and believe me, that woman could outtalk a radio. The only event I wasn't sure of was the raft contest, which was gonna be a difficult one to call. It took quite a dog, a dog with lots of grit, to swim out to that raft in the middle of Wilson's pond, grab a thirty-pound coon and then drag that mad sucker off into the water and pull him back to shore. Several dogs almost drowned last year in the event, and few of the hunters were willing to put their good coonhounds to the test. When the dogs made their grab for the coon he mounted their heads and the rodeo was on. It's hard to swim or catch your breath with thirty pounds of mad coon clinging with a death hold onto your ears. I figured that maybe the dogs had smartened up some. Like I heard a man say, you probably couldn't have melted most of them hounds and poured them onto that raft with that varmint. No sir, one dose of that raft deal was enough to dissuade all but the grittiest. On flat hard ground them hounds were more than willing to tackle old mister coon, but the water gave all the advantage to their opponent. Considering the situation I can't say I blame them much.

Pa would always attend the festivities to laugh and listen to the coon hunting stories from the past year but none of his dogs had ever participated in the daytime activities. Everyone in the county knew who had the best dogs in Blue Bottoms, so they weren't too terribly upset when Pa's dogs stayed home. Saturday night was the big finish as the men all drew out for the coon hunting contest. The storekeepers in Milburn donated a small purse for the winner. Pa wasn't no braggard like most coon hunters, but I don't think he minded folks around the country a knowing who had the best coonhounds in Johnston County. So as a result, RC was allowed to hunt Quane in the night hunt. Pa figured that was what real coon hunting was all about, putting the meat in the tree.

Well Saturday was two days away and tonight we were going hunting. RC promised to take me, and he never went back on his word. Quane would stay behind tonight, tied in the yard resting her up some and making her more eager than ever to hunt. Me, I didn't know of a dog except Rover that could outdo her on a track. She sure wasn't the fleetest of foot. When she got herself astraddle of a track, hot or cold, she was accurate and she was steady. When she barked "tree", the old gal had the meat for a fact. She had already won the night hunt two years in a row, and I had most of my marbles on her for this year. Only time I ever knew her not to have a coon when she treed was once, then she had two. No, she would occasionally miss a coon, but most times we couldn't see it up in the tall tree, or it had gotten itself into a hole. Like the man said one night, she was foolproof.

Well school was out for the day and here I stood finishing up the egg washing. I was daydreaming about hunting as usual, something that kept me in lots of trouble. RC and Pa were filling up the carbide lights, night was falling and the coons would soon be walking. Tonight would have a bite of cold, dark as a piece of coal ten feet down, and still as a dead log. A perfect night for coon hunting, shoot I don't think there was any other kind myself, but this one was the exception. Anyway, a coon hunter couldn't ask for more.

Slipping on my coat, I looked to where Granny sat candling her eggs. Granny was special, when in her presence you felt you were truly loved and at that moment she had a way of making you feel like you were the only person around. Yes, she was a grand lady, she always had time for you and she showed it. You know, one year we were studying about a Queen far away over the ocean in England. Sitting in that classroom, I pictured Granny, to all of us she was truly our queen. I almost felt guilty leaving her here with Joann working over the eggs while we were off hunting and enjoying ourselves. If I asked her if she wanted me to stay, she would only smile in her quiet way and tell me to go and have a good time. Yes, Granny was special, soft, and gentle. I never once seen her mad, maybe a little upset when I was shooting at her prize laying hens with my Red Ryder BB Rifle, but never really mad. I 'spect she was the only one who didn't get really mad at me.

Rover struck first as we made our way to the crossing on Blue. Tim, Jess, and George Dunn met us on the road to the crossing. They wanted to cut across to the foot log across Blue, but Pa didn't trust the old log. It would have cut off quite a long walk, but we continued to the crossing. That foot log had been there for many a year and was okay for the younger boys to cross, but Pa, well he was a big man and to him that old log didn't look too solid at all.

Rover and Fanny were really burning up the track. The way they were running, we figured they'd wind up in Filmore before they treed.

Fanny could flat out run a coon providing she didn't hit a coyote track and quit us cold. It were a gospel fact, she turned off on a hot wolf track more than once and left us holding the bag. Now Pa, he swore he was gonna swap her off every time she done it, but we still had her. Each time we went out hunting, we were a hoping she'd stick with the coon track.

Tonight we were in luck; them dogs ran due north away from the river and really opened it up crossing over some flat pastureland. I took off behind RC as fast as my short legs could motivate. Now Pa had tried to get me to stay back with him, but I was addicted, I just had to get to where the action was. When them dogs went to bawling and running, it made my legs start jumping around, and I just had to go. Couldn't help myself, no sir, I should have been a coonhound myself. I figure I missed my calling and maybe I did at that.

I had done worked myself up a sweat and was lagging far behind RC and the Dunn's boys when my foot went ear deep in some kind of varmint hole. Me and my carbide light went flopping out across the ground where we separated company. There I sat in the pitch dark, spitting out a mouthful of dirt, and feeling around for my light. Finally, after what seemed like several minutes, I managed to locate the dat burn thing and get it cleaned off. Now if it would only light. Sometimes them carbides had a mind of their own and could be downright contrary. Lucky for me tonight it was in a good mood, lighting right up as soon as I struck a match to her. That little old flame came alive and sent a nice beam of light straight out in front of me about twenty feet I reckon, and that's where the wreck took place.

Standing right there smack-dab in front of me was G.O. Jackson's Hereford bull, yep the same critter that had dealt me misery for the last couple of years. I'll tell you, I was on my feet before you could spit and praying for my feet not to fail me as I lit a shuck out of there. I didn't know if that bull was after me or not, I wasn't looking back. My bouncing carbide light illuminated a climbable tree. I shot over to it and took a good handhold on a low limb before looking back. Nothing, that bull was nowhere in sight, that sucker disappeared somewhere out in the dark.

My heart was beating faster than a hummingbirds wings as I stood there blowing air in and out like a wind broke horse. Man I sounded like a bellows down at the blacksmith shop, but I was in one piece. I never knew to this day why that rascal didn't wallow me all over that pasture. Catching my breath, I knew I wasn't out of the woods yet. It was pitch dark, I was a little turned around and wondering how far the fence was? Even if I made the fence, that bull was known to go through or over fences to chase people, and it was mainly me, he enjoyed chasing.

I wasn't about to yell out, no sir. If'n my mother, bless her soul, found out I was out here all alone with that bull keeping me company in the pitch dark, I'd probably never be allowed to go hunting again, ever. Nope, I was on my own. I got my fool self into this fix and I was for once gonna have to get myself out. Sounded good so far, but how was I gonna do it?

It was so dark, I couldn't see my hand in front of my face. The stars showed me which way the house was, that was no problem. I wasn't lost, I was treed. I needed to know which way the fence was, home right now wasn't gonna help me one bit. To top that off, my light was starting to sputter which meant it needed refilling. I had carbide in a snuff can in my pocket, but no water. Studying out how long I had been running before this mess came about, I knew I had to be west of the river, but how far west? Old Rover wasn't gonna be any help, he was like me. Coon hunting was his favorite pastime and right now I could hear him north of me burning up the track. Besides, he didn't know I was up to my ears in trouble again.

Well east it was, my light was running out, I had no choice. I was just fixing to launch myself out of there as fast as my feet could carry me when I heard a call from across the pasture. It was Pa hollering for Rover, from all the hollering and carrying on I figured that dang Hereford done up and had him treed. Now was the time to run while that sorry little bull was preoccupied with Pa. I wasn't abandoning Pa, no sir. I would bring Rover back to save him when I got safe myself. I couldn't see no reason for us both being mauled. Man I hit the ground running hard and was really toting the mail when wham, I ran smack-dab into that dat burned barbwire fence.

Talk about coming to a stop, that fence done flipped me backwards, shooting me like a stone out of my slingshot. By the time I got myself righted, I discovered my light had gone out, deader than a doornail. My pants were torn; shoot I looked like I had been in a fight with a bobcat. Well one good thing I reckon, I sure 'nuff found the fence or it had found me. Picking what was left of myself up off the ground I felt my legs and arms to see if I had any broken parts. Finding myself intact, I stared off into the dark and listened. Pa was still hollering for old Rover, so I figured that old bull was still keeping him company.

Now, all I had to do was follow the fence south back to the river and get my light watered up and relit, and then I would try to get Pa out of his predicament. For once I knew me and my conniving wasn't responsible for this mess. Just to be on the safe side, I rolled under the fence and started south. Now I wouldn't admit to being scared but I was a bit nervous. I could swear I smelled that dang bull. Then from the other side of that fence, I heard the unmistakable sound of something big and heavy walking along the other side keeping step with me.

That sorry sucker smelled me out and was now stalking me. I knew one thing for a fact; he wasn't showing me the way to the river. At least he was on the other side of the fence and now maybe Pa had a chance of getting away himself. I figured I would stay close to the fence because that little old bull was known to jump a fence and if he did, I figured to switch sides. Leastways I'd keep the sorry sucker jumping back and forth. Well it seemed like a mighty long walk banging into bushes and thorns, but finally I heard it, the unmistakable sound of the ripples running across the rocks of the crossing.

I couldn't help but shake my head disgustedly. I was in the upper cornfield, all I would have had to do was get ten feet away from the fence and I would have clear walking. Feeling my way down to the river, I filled the carbide, struck a match, and smiled in delight as the little light flickered to life. Man what a feeling of relief, I was saved. Leastways if Jackson's bull was gonna mangle me, I'd be able to see him coming.

I had my light burning and was fixing to go to Pa's relief when he came walking up. We stood there our ears straining, listening to the race when we finally heard the unmistakable sound of the hounds coming back our way. Poor old Pa, he looked like he had been in as much trouble as I had been. His clothes were torn and rough looking and he looked disheveled. Reminded me of the way I looked after one of my Saturday trips to Milburn. I didn't mention anything at all about the Hereford as he knelt down and got himself a drink of water.

The race ended kinda funny, them dogs ran up and treed within fifty feet of where we stood. RC and Tim came running up a few minutes later all out of breath and looking at us in disbelief. Oh we treed the coon alright, but the bull treeing us was never mentioned by me or Pa. To this day, I don't know if he knew I was in the same predicament as he was, I never mentioned it, and neither did he. We never did figure out where George and Jess had gotten off to until they came strolling up. I wondered if that bull treed them too. They never said either way but they both looked a little tuckered.

Anyway we had worn ourselves out and were ready to call it a night. We didn't even bother to look for the coon. RC led out straight south towards the house and after a mile or so we all wound up at that same old foot log that we had bypassed earlier. Now Pa was tired, the house was just a hop and a skip across the river, and that log was the fastest way to a warm fire. George walked out on the log and jumped up and down a few times declaring that old oak log was sound as a dollar. Now I never had many of them dollars, so I wouldn't know so much about their being sound. I figured the log was safe enough as I crossed it many a time, so I tore out following the rest of the boys.

Only Pa was left on the other side of the creek casting a critical eye across the water. At this point Old Blue wasn't deep but it was sure cold. We lifted the lanterns high trying to cast more light on the situation as Pa started inching his way across. So far everything seemed to be going just fine. Pa was about halfway across with all of us and Rover anxiously watching his progress. All of a sudden, I seen that log wiggle and then move a little. Pa froze but he was too late that old log rolled completely over flipping Pa and his lantern headfirst into the water. Sputtering and coughing as he came to the surface, he stood there drenched in waist deep water. I 'spect George and Jess had been nipping at a bottle cause they took one look at Pa and couldn't help but laugh. Poor old Pa, it sure hadn't been his night, first the bull, now the river.

Not a peep came from me or RC, we knew better. After Pa waded to shore, we managed to pull him up onto dry ground where Rover whined and wagged his tail. It was sure 'nuff cold, Pa was soaked to the bone and freezing, so we tore out for home. Jess and George finally stopped laughing and were patting Pa on the shoulder. Finally, I heard him chuckle a little himself. He was cold but the whole thing was over. Now it was funny, providing he didn't freeze himself to death or catch pneumonia. I couldn't help but wonder if Pa was gonna seek revenge against Mister Jackson's Hereford. Nah, Pa wasn't the kind to carry a grudge, tomorrow it would all be forgotten. Not me, pay back would have been swift and justice would have been served if he was the cause of me falling in the river. Now, I ain't saying he never put me in the water, he had, but it wasn't freezing out either. We sure had us a good story to tell around the old wood stove this winter.

Saturday was here, the day of the big coon meet and night hunt. Quane acted like she knew it, the same as I did. I was still sore from falling in that hole, and that dang fence trying to strangle me. I was young so I healed up pretty quick. On the other hand Pa was still getting around mighty slow, but for once I was keeping my mouth shut. During breakfast RC kept casting a curious glance at me and Pa from time to time, I think he suspected we were hiding something, but he never asked.

Finished with breakfast and our morning chores, we headed for Wilsons for the big doings. The Shico Farm was about a half mile or so west of Egypt schoolhouse, up a sandy road. Sandy, that was stretching it a little, that had to be the sandiest farm in the county, but it sure would grow the peanuts. I've still got some of that sand in my mouth from standing around the thrashing machine while the men were sacking Wilson's peanuts.

It looked like everyone in the county was already there. There were wagons and trucks parked everywhere. Every one of them had dogs in them, on them, or tied to them. I had never seen so many dogs in one place. RC already threatened me with my life, no fighting, marble shooting, and no slingshot. How did he expect a body to enjoy himself?

You'd a thought, the way he was threatening me with bodily harm that I was a troublemaker. Well I finally gave my word, shucks I would have promised anything to go to this hoedown cause I knew it was gonna be a doozy. Plus the fact, I just knew I was fixing to win me some marbles.

I was all bug eyed as I walked in among them hounds. I knew most everybody there, some were strangers but very few. I left my best marbles and slingshot home. Confound it my mouth went with me but I was doing my best to keep it shut. My good friend Tommy McGlaughlin was there, he was my age but that was all we had in common. I was kinda a normal puny little kid, whereas Tommy well let's just say he didn't miss many meals. Yes sir, he was a head higher and probably thirty or forty pounds heavier than me. Tommy had a bad temper and many a day if we didn't have anyone else to fight, we'd just tear into each other but we were still friends. Walking side by side, me and old Tommy passed through the place looking all those hounds over with a critical eye.

Then it was on to our next attraction, which was Mrs. Shico's kitchen. We stuffed our pockets with her sugar cookies and then thanking her we were on our merry way. Pearl was Wilson's wife. The most kindly woman besides Granny, I ever knew. She had a booming laugh that seemed to wake the neighborhood. Me or nobody I ever knew left her house hungry, Pearl was one of a kind. I swear she had the smallest kitchen. You'd sit there eating on a summer day just sweating away cause that old wood cookstove wasn't five feet away. Besides Granny's vittles, hers was the tastiest I ever wrapped myself around.

They were a pair, Wilson was a short Choctaw and Pearl was a big grey haired lady, taller than Wilson. They were without a doubt the cream of the crop. No sir, no finer neighbors or friends ever existed.

We walked back to where the dogs were. I was on cloud nine and this was my kind of a show. There were treeing contests, coon squalling contests, swimming contests, and last but not least, the raft contest. Oh, I almost forgot there was the barrel contest. I noticed the barrel right off but didn't see anything around it. A fair sized chain was wrapped around a stake in front of the barrel and the other end was running into the barrel. The inside of that can was pitch black; I couldn't see a thing in there.

Now being a busybody came natural to me, I was naturally the curious type. Well sir, I leaned over and was gonna take a gander at whatever was in that barrel when the hair raisingest growl I ever heard came from within that dark hole. About that time the man who turned out to be the owner of that thing snatched me back by my arm, almost dislocating the dang thing at my shoulder.

It turned out that chain was hooked on the other end to the meanest, toothiest, blackest looking Lynx Cat I ever seen; well I reckon he was a Lynx Cat, as he was the only one I had actually ever seen. I didn't get to see much of him, leastways not at first with that man a yanking on me like I was a catfish on a hook. I wasn't gonna hurt his old cat, just wanted to see him was all. RC was glaring at me from where he stood but I was used to that. Seemed like everybody glared at me for one reason or another.

Anyway, the man had him a moneymaking enterprise going with that dang wildcat and the half-buried barrel. The whole idea of the scheme was anybody could put up five dollars to try to win fifty. It was simple and fairly easy, at least it was to hear the man explain it. All one had to do was wager five bucks then sic his unsuspecting hound on that bundle of razor blades inside the barrel. If the dog pulled the Lynx out he won the fifty dollars. Sounds simple enough alright, that is if the cat went along with the idea, which he probably wasn't likely to do.

Let me tell you, that thing had teeth four inches long, toenails even longer, and a temper even longer than that. Only thing he didn't have was a tail and the way he was backed up in that barrel, I didn't reckon he needed one of those. He went through every dog they sicced in there quicker than water through a sieve. Oh they'd make a run at the barrel, but one good look at that thing, or a good raking with them claws, would be all they wanted. They'd stand in front of that barrel, bark their heads off, and that was it. They weren't fixing to endanger their bodies going in after that thing. I saw right off, once a hound shied back and went to barking, he was finished fighting. You could sic'em all you wanted, but you couldn't melt them hounds and pour them back into that barrel. Was kinda funny though watching and listening, when the men seen their five dollars disappear down the pocket of the cat man. They'd get mad and go to cussing their dogs for cowards. I'll bet you it would have taken a lot of Jess' moonshine to get nary one of them fellers to climb into that barrel themselves.

Oh I forgot to mention, there was a time limit and the unsuspecting dog had to pull that thing outta the barrel within five minutes. Shucks five minutes, or five hours, it was all the same. It only took most of them dogs about five seconds to figure out they were needed somewhere else and that wasn't on the working end of them long sharp claws.

RC stood watching the proceedings and I knew for a fact that devious little mind of his was working on some scheme. I'd seen it in the thinking mode too many times not to recognize it. His eyebrows would come together, then he'd get that little sneaky grin on his face, yep there it were, he was up to something sure 'nuff. Fifty dollars was a whole lot of money, more than I could even imagine. I was right, it wasn't long before he and Charlie Dunn had their heads together and were definitely plotting something. I jabbed Tommy in the stomach as Charlie left outta there like a turpentined tomcat.

Something was fixing to happen, I knew RC all too well. Pulling me up a piece of shade I reached for a cookie and waited. I wasn't gonna miss whatever he was up to, no sir. Sure enough it weren't long before old Charlie came trotting back with his mother's old dog. Now that Collie was once a real cow dog but he was old, way too old to be getting himself mixed up fighting that wildcat. I could tell by the worried look in his eye he felt the same way. I don't reckon I ever seen a dog with hair as long as that Collie had hanging from him.

That wasn't the worst of it, when Mrs. Dunn found out they had her pet dog down here fighting, well I for one didn't want to miss out on that show either. She was a quiet, dignified lady but I'm a betting if she knew about what they were fixing to get her pet dog into, she probably would have got a little vocal, to say the least. She thought more of that old dog than she did Charlie, can't say I blame her there. Shucks the old Collie wasn't even asked to run the cows anymore, he was retired. For a fact it sure didn't matter now, the dog was here and the cat was in the barrel. RC had his five dollars in his hand and the fifty dollars on his devious little mind.

Well, while the palavering between RC and the man was going on, I spotted Delmar with his Daddy standing a few feet away. I had already bet all my marbles on the upcoming contests, so I borrowed ten marbles from Tommy and lit a shuck over there to place my bet. I knew old Delmar had been watching that thing chew up and spit out everything in sight. Dogs a whole lot bigger and stronger than the Collie hadn't lasted until the water got hot as they said, so I figured he'd be a sucker for an easy bet. He had already seen how bad that little old cat was. What he didn't know too much about was RC was as devious as that Lynx Cat was vicious.

The fighting was finished, over, done. Nobody else in the crowd wanted to wager their money knowing it was like throwing it down a deep well. Sure enough old Delmar jumped right on my bet. I showed him my marbles and he showed me his. Delmar and I fought many a time over marbles so we needed what they called a neutral party to hold our wager. Delmar didn't trust Tommy, can't say I blamed him there even though Tommy was my best friend. We finally decided to let Collie McGlaughlin, Tommy's Dad hang on to them after we made sure he understood the bet.

I walked back to where Tommy waited, a big grin splashed across my innocent little face, watching as RC gave the man his money. Taking the Collie's rope from Charlie, RC gave me a hard look then walked over in front of the barrel. I'd seen that look before, I reckon after seeing the grin on my face he figured I was up to something.

Jess Dunn had been watching the proceedings kinda halfhearted or half drunk can't say which. When he spied the Collie in RC's grasp, he came alive like he'd been lightning struck and started towards the barrel. Charlie interceded and got his uncle slowed down long enough for RC to spring Mrs. Dunn's poor old dog on that barrel of meanness. Several of the men sitting around in the shade started snickering and roaring with laughter, which I thought, would make RC mad but he only grinned.

I slipped around trying to look inside that barrel best I could. All I could see was a pair of evil eyes looking back out at me, eyes that reminded me of them dat burned water moccasins in the river. That thing sure didn't look none too concerned to me, why should he, armed from talon to tooth with razor sharp weapons? He'd done whipped everything in sight and he hadn't even worked up a good sweat. Shucks, most of them hounds ran up to that barrel ready to tackle anything but after one or two swipes they backed up and went to barking at that thing. Then it was all over and I can't say I blamed them. I sure wasn't about to stick my head in there, no siree bob, I liked my face just like it was.

RC had to carry and drag the old Collie over to the barrel. I don't think the poor thing wanted to participate in this little fiasco at all. I sure didn't see any way that poor old dog was fixing to pounce on that bag of teeth and claws voluntarily like. Worried me some to, I was kinda worried about my marbles already. Of course I had faith in RC, I knew he was probably more unscrupulous than the cat owner when it came to a bet, as he wasn't fixing to lose five dollars.

Well it was too late to call the bet off even if old Delmar would have, which he wouldn't. I hardly blinked twice when the cat feller looked at his pocket watch and nodded. Quicker than a gopher could dig a hole, RC grabbed that poor Collie up and stuffed him rear end first into that barrel. About the time the Lynx Cat grabbed him a good hold on that Collie's hind end, the dog let out a terrified scream. RC up and jerked the dog, wildcat, chain and all out of that barrel. That poor old dog was a hollering and screaming in mortal terror while the wildcat was hissing and growling. The crowd was whooping and hollering but the man with the wildcat was hollering even louder.

Not RC, he just stood there calm as could be, waiting on his money. The wildcat owner was red faced and livid, hollering foul. He knew he had been had and was refusing to cough up the fifty dollars. I just shook my head and grinned, RC had done it again. I done told Tommy he was devious. I could have told the wildcat man that too, as I had been on the losing end of that brain to many times.

The man jumped up and down, claiming he had been cheated. Hardly anyone was listening because most lost money to the feller already. RC said he never touched the wildcat, which nobody in their right mind would, so there had been no foul play. Well it was nip and tuck there for awhile but RC wasn't backing down as he was well thought of in this country. As the man looked around at the surrounding hunters who moved in closer, he decided the odds were against him and handed over the money.

Last I seen, the man, barrel, and wildcat were headed back to wherever they came from. The poor old Collie, when Charlie turned him loose, I swear I didn't think he had it in him; he left there like a cyclone headed due east towards home. I doubt he ever knew what had taken hold of his hind side, but for sure he didn't want any more of it. He hadn't been hurt as long as his hair was. I still didn't figure Charlie was gonna get off scot-free when Mrs. Dunn found about her prize dog fighting for his life. The dog was petrified almost out of his wits and scared out of two years of his life. I knew Jess Dunn was drinking and laughing and I knew he'd have to tell this story. Poor old Charlie, oh well, if RC split even with him, I guess half the money was worth a few smacks on the backside. You know, I never did figure how that feller got the collar and chain around that thing's neck without getting ate up or I might have tried it myself. Looked like a moneymaking proposition to me, leastways until RC came along and spoiled it.

That only left the raft contest to finish off the day before the big coon hunt that night. Quane, she was laying up at home, saving her energy for the exertion she was fixing to have to put out later, course she didn't know she was resting.

The coon hunters had them a raft out on the middle of Wilson's pond with a coon sitting right dab in the middle of it. It seemed like a simple enough contest, all a dog had to do was swim out there, coax the coon off that raft and swim with it back to the shore. Now I didn't mention the fact that the coon on that raft was one of the biggest coons I had ever seen and I had seen a few. If I'd been the coon, I'd of tried to beat a hasty retreat out of there but with all the people and dogs surrounding the pond there was no place to retreat to. He already figured out the raft was the safest place for him.

Now I'd seen this same coon and raft the last two years, several men dang near got their hounds drowned trying to land Mister Ringtail. Most had smartened up and left their good hounds tied where they were. Some others got smart and brought some kind of worthless fighting dog for the contest, a trick that didn't faze old mister Coon one bit. A coon is a natural swimmer and will climb up on a dogs head, get him a good stranglehold and drown the poor hound deader than a doornail.

Well I still had a cookie or two left and a ringside seat on that pond dam. This was gonna be a show for sure, a real jim-dandy, dang near better than a Roy Rodgers and Trigger movie. Last year besides the dogs fighting the coon, there were several owners fighting one another. I ain't never figured out which is better, people fighting or a dog and coon fighting. It is kinda funny watching two potbellied men, huffing and puffing, wrestling around on the ground. Me, I done swore when my stomach began to stick out more than my arms I was gonna give up fighting altogether. Yes sir, things were starting to liven up around Wilson's old farm for sure. If I didn't miss my guess it was gonna be a hot time in the old house tonight. Ain't nothing like watching two critters fighting to get men in the mood to fight themselves, just natural I reckon.

The first dog brought forth was a rearing to go; the idgit spotted the coon a prancing around on the raft and took off swimming in hot pursuit. Man the dog was all excited, leastways until he tried pulling himself on that raft and that coon charged, getting himself a good mouth full of soft dog nose. It sure didn't take long for that dog to vacate the premises and exit the pond. That old coon watched as the dog retreated, then sat on the small raft and looked out at everybody. Funny thing was, when that hound got back up on dry ground, all of a sudden his nerve came back. He stood there his hackles up and a barking, but his owner couldn't hiss him back in the water. What a show, dogs were barking, people hollering and laughing at the disappointed dog owner. Then just as calm as a cucumber that old coon reached down and got himself a good drink of pond water and then waited on his next victim. No sir, he sure wasn't too concerned about his health.

These weren't coon dogs; most had never really seen a coon in the wild. The next dog was a boxer dog of some kind but he didn't fare any better. He swam out there alright but I reckon the coon was a bit riled. He up and baled off on that poor dog and dang near drowned the poor sucker before he could get loose and beat a hasty retreat. Well I could see right quick this wasn't going no place, that coon had the deadwood on them dogs and he wasn't leaving that raft. I watched almost bored, a cookie sticking from my mouth, counting to myself, two down.

Well wouldn't you know it, my eyes almost bugged out, here came RC again and walking along beside him was none other than old Rover. I knew this was fixing to be the boy's Waterloo, I learned that word out of a schoolbook too. This had to be the last straw; Pa was fixing to skin my poor uncle, providing he didn't beat him to death first. My mind was thinking so fast of all the bad things that were fixing to happen to RC when Pa found out. Rover was in this mess, I didn't even realize I ate all my cookies. I just kept chewing on thin air and swallowing. I could see it all now, Mrs. Dunn beating on poor Charlie and Pa strapping RC, this could turn out downright interesting to say the least.

Wouldn't you know it, just when I had all the possibilities figured out on blackmailing the boys for a few marbles, here comes Pa as big as life. He takes the lead rope that's around Rover's neck. Now I was shocked, why would Pa put Rover onto the raft coon when he had been so against it the last two years? Later I found out, some of the local coon hunters had told last week in Milburn that they bet Rover didn't have the guts to get that old coon. Pa wasn't about to let them call his dog a coward, no sir, after all, Rover had his reputation to uphold. Well I doubt Rover cared one way or another about his reputation but Pa was gonna uphold it for him anyway. Course now Pa wasn't fixing to be the one swimming out there and getting thirty pounds of riled up coon off that raft.

Anyhoo, Pa walked down to the water's edge and let Rover see the coon out there walking back and forth on that raft like he owned it. I reckon he did at that, at least temporarily. Things got deathly quiet around that pool of water except for the barking dogs that is. Not a murmur came from the crowd, all the bets had been placed, now they were all on their feet standing around the pond watching. Rover's reputation was well known by most of the spectators, but that coon was big, and he had everything in his favor. I hadn't collected my marbles from Delmar yet or I would have wagered some more on Rover.

I noticed RC removed his shoes just in case Rover might need a little assistance. There was no way Pa was going to let that dog of his get himself drowned, reputation or not. Well if it came down to it and poor old RC had to fight that thing out in the water, I'd bet my money on RC. The boy could swim like a fish, and when riled, he had the temperament of an alligator. I already knew that poor coon was whipped, trouble was he didn't know it.

Sure 'nuff, Pa hissed Rover and in that water he went. It was a sight, they still tell about today. Rover didn't try to fight, he just swam up alongside that raft and old Mister Coon baled out on top of him, grabbed a handful of red hair and hung on. Just as calm as a Baptist Preacher in church, Rover paddled that critter right over to dry ground and proceeded to give Mister Coon a good baptizing. Short and sweet, that was the end of the raft show for the day. I couldn't say for sure whether the other coon hunters were happy with the results or not. One thing was sure, if they didn't already know about the big red dog, they sure enough knew who he was now. Old Rover went home with even a

bigger reputation than he already had. Both Pa and RC had their chests
thrown out proudly and both were a lot richer.

Oh, and Quane won the night hunt treeing three coons, it was a
good day all around. I was still wondering when Mrs. Dunn was going
to tie into Charlie but I guess she never did. At least I never heard
anything and I never missed anything if I could help it.

My pockets were filled to the brim with marbles and would have
been more if'n I'd known Pa was gonna let Rover in on the fun. Oh well,
I reckon a person shouldn't be greedy.

Chapter 16
The Egg Incident

It was fall again and the days were starting to get shorter. We just started back to school and believe it or not, I managed to pass another grade for this school year. My good friend Thaddeus moved away to Tulsa with his folks. Sadly, the old schoolhouse didn't seem the same without him and his thick glasses.

Joann got herself promoted into high school so now she rode the school bus to Milburn. I think with all her brains, Almond our teacher skipped her through a couple of grades so she landed there early. Yep, she got to ride the bus and stick her tongue out at us less fortunate ones as we plodded down the dusty road to school.

Back in them days, us younger kids weren't allowed to ride the half-empty bus, no matter if it were raining, storming, snowing, or if a pack of wolves were chasing us. It wasn't fair, Christian or Democratic; leastways I didn't think it was. There sure weren't no use crying over spilled milk, sides there wasn't no one left to tell on me if'n I got in a fight or got caught doing something I wasn't supposed to do. You sure couldn't play marbles on a school bus.

Funny thing about that telling stuff, we didn't have a telephone, don't reckon I even knew what one was, but somehow or another Pa always knew if we had been in trouble in school before we got home. I never could figure that one, I thought maybe he was psychic, learned that word in school too.

My Aunt Sylvia went to live with Aunt Wynona somewhere in Texas and she latched herself onto a brand shiny new husband. Now that wasn't bad enough, he was a Yankee and a sailor all tied up in one. We thought he was a pirate or something exciting like that, but nah, no such luck. When I first laid eyes on him, he had both his arms and no peg leg, shucks he didn't even have a parrot, nothing. On top of that, he was a city slicker from Bethlehem, Pennsylvania, wherever that is. Well sure enough, they showed up on the farm one weekend and everyone was making a fuss over this funny talking fellow. Me and Rover, we retreated out of sight and hearing while all the introducing and handshaking was going on. What a disappointment, the guy was definitely no pirate.

You talk about a city dude and green, why he didn't know come here from sic'em. Me and Rover were sitting on the front porch the first day they arrived watching Charles, which was his name. Anyway, we were watching him walk around and around the house looking in every room and every closet. He seemed a little anxious. Finally, he stopped smack-dab in front of us with that silly looking grin on his face and asked where the bathroom was.

Now I thought he wanted to take a bath in the middle of the day. Come to find out that wasn't what he wanted at all. He was a wanting the outhouse. I'd never heard it called a bathroom before. Anyway, I pointed him towards the river but thankfully, he didn't get that far before Sylvia cut him off and pointed him out back. You talk about a confused look on a man's face as he started out the back door. I was wandering to myself, where in the world did he think an outhouse would be.

Charles was a character to say the least, always smiling, laughing, and wanting to help. Trouble was he was a city boy, around a farm he was dumb as a box of rocks. He meant well though, it's just you can't get milk from a cow by pumping her tail like he thought. Leastways he knew where the outhouse was now. I was just a wondering what was gonna happen first time he ran into a rattlesnake on his way there or into G.O. Jackson's sweet natured little bull. I was a figuring to myself how that little wreck might come about; real innocent of course; I sure didn't want to miss it. Now a harmless little old Blue Racer Snake might do the trick. Them things were harmless but if you didn't know it, they'd sure scare the dickens out of you. Course now if I got caught, I'd be in big trouble. Aunt Sylvia had a terrible temper and she wasn't about to let anything human or animal mess with her Charles.

Sylvia and Charles arrived on Friday and Saturday was always washday for Granny and the girls. Driving the wagon and water barrels down to the crossing on Blue to fill the rain barrels was mostly my job. RC gathered wood and started the fire. The team was hitched and I was all set to leave out when Charles lands himself in the seat beside me. Now our horses were gentle and could almost get the water by themselves, they had done it so much. Naturally Charles wanted to drive the wagon, so I handed over the lines and got myself a death grip on the wagon, cause I figured this wasn't gonna work out well at all. It was a wreck fixing to happen, that's what it was. I swear that boy could wreck an anvil, but I had to admit he'd be smiling all the while he was doing it. Charles was harmless and he was friendly as all get out, but man was he green, shucks he invented the word.

Pa himself, the he hog and boss of the outfit was standing right there watching the proceedings. He didn't say nary a word, nothing, and it were his wagon and horses. I thought I saw RC make a cross on himself as we went by. I knew he wasn't Catholic or anything like that. Shoot, he wasn't even religious or he wouldn't have always been giving me the dickens. I do believe RC was one of those heathen fellers, who normally accompanied me to the river bailed out of the wagon as soon as he seen Charles take the lines. I ain't joking, Charles climbed in and Rover climbed out.

Well believe it or not, we made the river in one piece and I took the lines from Charles and backed the wagon down into the shallows. I'll say one thing old Charles was willing to work; trouble was he didn't know how. He jumped in the back and grabbed up a bucket, which was fine with me, yes sir he was nimble and willing. He was a filling them barrels lickity-split while I was sitting there out of the way giving him all the room he needed. I was pretty good at letting someone else do my work if they were of a mind to. Weren't any use arguing with the boy, he was determined. Finally, in about half the time it would have took me, them barrels were full so we started back to the house to fill up the large cast iron wash pots. Now the Saturday washing needed a lot of water, it took two loads, so we had to go after another one for rinse water.

Charles informed me he would go get the next load by himself while I tended the fire. As usual RC skedaddled somewhere, he hated washday. Well, off old Charlie boy went, and I occupied myself with aggravating Joann and Sylvia. Thirty minutes passed and no Charles, then Sylvia began to fret. Now I'll tell you Sylvia was as sweet as anything unless she got her dander up then look out. She could outfight a wampus wildcat, and that ain't no joke. Now fretting that was her main bragging point, when she up and got herself nervous look out, here came the fretting. Her new found husband was missing and she wasn't about to lose him. Don't know what she thought would get him down on the river; we didn't have any grizzly bear or alligators in these parts. Anyway, we were all headed for the river in high gear to find what was left of poor Charles, except Granny that is. I figure she thought like me, he was in the navy, how could water hurt him? She never budged from the wash fires.

There was no reason to hurry. Shoot, there was no way that he could get hurt just driving that wagon down to the crossing for water. Wrong again, we all took the short cut to the river. When we walked out on what was left of the railroad trestle, lo and behold there sat Charles on the wagon bed hanging onto a tree limb. The rest of the wagon and the horses were still standing at the crossing. RC just shook his head, Charles had driven off into a deep hole of water that I neglected to tell him about. That wood wagon bed somehow came untied and just up and floated down stream.

I reckon I do remember telling him as he drove away on his trip to the river; that he needed to get into a little deeper water to make the loading easier. That would make the water closer to the barrels; well it sure did do that. One barrel was still in the water but I didn't see the other and that was something to really fret over. If one of Pa's good barrels was lost under water somebody was gonna get a thrashing and that somebody was probably gonna be poor little old me.

I could tell by the way RC was glaring at me, even though I was pretending innocence that I was in for it when everybody turned their backs. Next thing I know I was hitting the river head first, he'd done up and threw me off the trestle. It wasn't even my fault; leastways I didn't think it was entirely.

Well after I nearly drowned myself, we got the wagon back in one piece, and all the clothes were washed and hanging on the line. So far, I was in one piece just a little wetter, besides my clothes needed washing anyway. Luckily, the other barrel went aground on a sand bar so my hindsight was still intact, at least for now.

Saturday week came and Granny had herself a wagonload of eggs ready to go to town, plus several pounds of butter, and we still had old Charles with us. Now Granny shipped her eggs in boxes of twelve dozen all stacked on top one another. Take my word for it that was a lot of work involved in selling eggs. Washing, candling, and packing them things, not to mention churning that butter. Now there was a job for a fact, working that old churn or shaking a quart jar back and forth until the butter formed. Not a blemish showed on nary an egg, nope, not one imperfection. Most of the time we had a full wagon load of eggs and butter to sell, providing that is, we didn't have an egg-sucking dog hanging around.

Like I said before, Granny was as gentle as a spring breeze except when it came to her eggs. Nothing, dog, snake, varmint, or kids had better mess with her egg production because she wouldn't tolerate it. Granny didn't stand much over five feet tall and a lot of her chicken nests were old wore out washtubs hanging head high in a tree. Granny favored the white leghorn type laying machine, them things could fly like a bird, reaching them high nests were no problem at all for them hens. The idea was to keep our hounds from getting the eggs. One evening me and Joann were shelling corn to feed the chickens while Granny gathered the eggs. Now she didn't bring her eggs in with a lard can, no sir, we brought them things in by the bucket full.

Anyway, Granny she up and reached above her head and started feeling around for eggs and I just happened to be watching. Next thing I knew she came out of that washtub with a six-foot long hog snake wrapped around her arm and he weren't none too happy. Man them things always gave me the willies. That old snake was a mite upset. Granny interrupted his dinner and she was a mite upset that he dared eat her precious eggs. Calm as a dead squirrel she looks that ugly thing in the eye and totes him over to the chopping block. Whack, which was the end of Mister Snake's egg sucking days. I could have warned him what was fixin' to happen. Granny had grit, I'll give her that, been me I'd got the shotgun and peppered that snake, nest and all. I don't cotton to snakes and I sure ain't about to reach blindly into a nest and shake hands with one.

Like I said, it was Saturday, which was egg-peddling day, normally RC's job unless Pa wanted to go to town. We had the wagon loaded, RC and Charles were on the seat and I was in the rear of the wagon. I wasn't about to miss the show. Being a mite on the nosey side, I was aching to see how the town people greeted a Yankee and a pirate. You know the Civil War wasn't so very far in the past. We were learning about that too in our schoolbooks. Now I've been in a few fights in my days and I ain't real bright. However, even a dummy like me could have told them Rebs they was a fixin' to get the snot kicked out of them. I mean when you're outnumbered twenty to one and the other side's got all the marbles, no sir looked like a losing proposition to me from the start, turned out that way too.

Waving as we drove out of the yard, I watched Sylvia staring after Charles like a lovesick calf that was never gonna see its mama again. Shucks, we were just going to town not a slaughterhouse, and that was only eight miles. I swear she acted like he was leaving the world. I expected her to start wailing at any minute, scare the mules, have a runaway, and break the eggs, but she didn't, would have been interesting though. I reckon she really cared for the boy. I would have liked him better if he had been a sure 'nuff ocean pirate with a hook for an arm, like in the picture shows.

Wouldn't you know it Charles wanted to drive so RC let him, now we done been down this road once already. Slipping closer to the tailgate, I was ready to evacuate the premises if he let the team run off or drove us over a cliff somewhere. Course now there were no cliffs anywhere near the county road but this was Charles driving, anything could happen. Our team of mules, well they weren't the most reliable; those things would run off at the drop of a hat. Old Tom and Roadie were notorious for tearing up things. Tom was gentle but that mare mule had rather run than eat, flighty, that's what Pa called her. Mule lovers always told how a mule would outwork a horse two to one and eat half the feed. Maybe they could but I personally never seen it. I knew one thing for a sure enough fact, them long eared cousins of a jackrabbit could tear up more in a day than you could put back together in a week. I've seen'em take the studs and just lay flat down and sull in their traces. Now, old Tom and Roadie weren't the sulling type, nope, they were the running kind, and old Charles our pirate, was a steering this ship.

Well for once, I'd be completely innocent if anything happened and right about then it did. Charles loved to talk and laugh, shoot you couldn't go squirrel hunting with him cause he'd scare all the critters away before we got to the woods. He couldn't help it; he just couldn't shut his mouth. Listening to him, I seen now how them Yankees whipped us; they flat talked us to death. Tom and Roadie were walking out pretty brisk. Their old ears just a keeping time in motion to their feet and Charles was gabbing and laughing when he made the fatal turn onto the county road. I guess he turned too short and the wheel hung. I wasn't watching, should have been though, next thing I knew them eggs and the rest of us were scattered smack-dab all over the bar ditch.

RC was a hollering whoa so loud here came Rover down the lane to get in on the fun. Fun, man I was picking stickers out of my backside and elbows, all the while eyeballing those egg crates, which were kinda deflated to say the least. Charles he's a hollering he's sorry, them mules were thinking on running, and RC he's trying to figure how to lay this mess on poor little old me. Now for once I was innocent on all counts like I heard the man say when they blamed him for hog stealing. Never could figure why he stole that hog anyway, dang thing was skinny as a rail post.

Anyway, with a little groaning we righted the wagon and hooked the team back up and believe it or not we only busted a few of Granny's eggs. We weren't going back to the house though, there were some things Granny sure didn't need to know. One thing happened though, after sending Rover back to the house, RC drove the rest of the way into town. Old Charles went back to the high seas the very next day. To top the day off, the same city folks who always wanted to bust my nose, treated Charles like they were glad to meet him. Yep, he up and made friends with everyone in town. Like I said, Charles was a talker and he was downright friendly.

You know he became a preacher after his pirating days on the high seas was over. Well I guess he never was a pirate, but I hinted to my school friends he was, shucks they'd never know the difference, they never met a real pirate. I'll bet, he made a dang good preacher, he was long-winded enough. All in all, it was an interesting visit but I think everyone was relieved the farm was still in one piece as our pirate drove off down the lane. Course now we hadn't seen the last of old Charles but we had seen more than enough of him for this summer.

Chapter 17
The Races

The warm sweet smell of springtime was again in the air and that meant only one thing, work. RC was in the fields plowing getting ready to plant, and I was sitting alongside the clods of black earth trying to outsmart a gopher the plow had unearthed. I was still a little small to hold up that twelve-inch walking plow so my main job was to keep RC working. Oh, I'd bring him a drink of creek water ever now and then when he hollered, which wasn't too often. RC wasn't much of a drinker himself. Now Uncle Howard, Wynona's Texas husband, yea another Texan, he could drink coffee from the time he got up till he went to bed, never seen the like. Aunt Wynona, we all called her Noni, picked her a good one in Howard. He worked hard and was a lot of fun to be around. Noni, she was like Granny, even reminded me of her. She looked like Granny, and had the same soft smile and kindness. Only thing, every time I got within spitting distance she wanted to wash my face or comb my hair, both of which I could do without. You know come to think of it, all of Granny and Pa's kids were sweet and good-natured most of the time. Well maybe Sylvia was a little hotheaded, but we all loved her. Floyd and Keith, my older uncles seldom ever lost their tempers. Uncle Floyd, who Keith had nicknamed Froggie D for some unknown reason, was really good-natured. Keith every now and then, could get a little upset when provoked, but mostly he was mild mannered as well. RC now, he was a little different egg altogether, like I've told you before.

Howard, he was skinny, I mean skinny, but that boy could jump and run. He could hold a broomstick in his hands and jump through it. That little trick always stuck in my mind. I tried it a time or two and almost broke my leg yep Howard was a jumper. Our mule Roadie could jump, but I'm a thinking Howard had her beat. He could run too, I remember him chasing RC around the house one time on the Fourth of July with a Roman Candle he had brought from Texas. We'd never seen many of them long tubes that just kept shooting off fire and popping noisily. Anyway Howard was in hot pursuit of RC and with all the noise, hollering, and fireworks every animal on the place jumping fences or running through them. Sure didn't make Pa none too happy.

All the hounds ran under the house, the chickens were in the trees, and the horses and cows were headed for the bottoms. July Fourth was a lot of fun, old Howard he was a corker, a lot of fun to be around and he sure did enjoy his coffee.

Getting back to the cornfield, that old plow, it was skimming through the black dirt, a scraping sound coming from it every time it plowed up a rock. Me and Rover were still digging for that mole. We caught sight of the critter a time or two and Rover would dig all the harder but we came up empty-handed each time. I heard RC holler whoa, so I left Rover in charge of the mole and hurried across the plowed field with my gallon jug of water wrapped with wet tow sacks and baling wire. Water and toting the overturned rocks from the field was my main job.

Those old mule's bellies were dripping water and I was thinking to myself they weren't gonna feel like running today. We were in the small cornfield near Blue Crossing. It was Saturday and I knew what RC had on his mind. The field was about half plowed and needed finishing. It still needed to be harrowed smooth before it was ready for the corn to be planted. Now there's where I came in, I was plenty big enough to ride a harrow. It just so happened there was a baseball game that afternoon over at Filmore, the first of the year and RC was aching to go.

Looking up at the sun, I judged it to be almost dinnertime. Now it was five miles cross country to the ball field, actually it was just a cow pasture but we played ball there anyway. If the ball landed in any kind of small pile, well you just dug it out and threw it home.

Them Choctaws over at Filmore could really play baseball and RC liked going over there. I dumped the rock and went back to my mole chasing as RC clucked to the mules and away they went. Now I knew what he was figuring, we'd plow till dinner then catch up a horse and ride to the game. That is providing Pa would let us. Pa was a stickler for keeping the Good Book Day; we never worked on Sunday other than our must do chores. However, today was Saturday, he sure 'nuff didn't have any problems with us working on Saturday.

RC hollered whoa and unhooked the team from the plow, leaving it sitting at the end of a row ready to start plowing when we returned. Walking the team to the river, he let them drink their fill all the time looking off towards Filmore. I really didn't figure Pa was gonna let us go to the ball game but I knew RC's mind was made up. Driving the team back to the house for dinner, we didn't unharness them. We pulled off their work bridles and pitched them six ears of corn, leaving them tied to the feed box eating contentedly.

Granny had a meal piled up on the long eating table that was fit for a king. Cornbread, okra, squash, pinto beans, fried taters, raw onions and plenty of sweet milk. You couldn't eat no better. I looked out to where the mules were chewing that hard corn and was sure glad I'd been born a human.

I pitched in and went to eating, but my ears stayed pointed, they were waiting for RC to spring it on Pa about the ball game. Now Pa, he'd been down in the east cornfield just a harrowing his little heart out and he hadn't unharnessed his team either. That was my first clue; I knew right then RC was out of luck. We weren't going to no ball game; the only place we were headed was straight back to plowing.

I figured this was gonna be a long afternoon so I dug in and fortified myself. Finally, RC got around to it and popped the question. Pa never missed a bite as he kept chewing but somehow the word no came out loud and clear. Now you can tell when RC would get himself a little perplexed or downright mad. Right now he was busy eating and he wasn't definitely sure Pa's no was the final decision. Well sir, the next no came out a lot louder and this time RC turned red. You can always tell when the boy was mad. His temples would go to jumping around, his eyes would get squinty, and right now, they were getting that way in a hurry. He was dead set on going, Pa was dead set on him not going and up and said so. Something was sure fixing to happen alright.

Not another word was said as we finished dinner and started back to the stomp lot. Pa grabbed his team and we put the work bridles back on the mules and started back. Handing the lines over to me, RC motioned for me to go on to the bottoms. I watched as he disappeared from sight, then I plodded on behind the mules towards the lower cornfield. The next time he showed himself, he had his ball, glove, bat, and he was riding his little black mare. I had me a very uneasy feeling; you know one of those we're in trouble feelings. My backsides were already starting to burn. Sure 'nuff, he tied the mules to an oak tree and we mounted Blackie and crossed the river. For some reason I had me a very nervous twitch down the middle of my back. There was no way Pa wouldn't know we weren't working the field, no sir. When Rover returned to where he was plowing and didn't leave him, our goose was cooked for sure. I was just wondering if I could plead I was too little to stop RC, but I reckon it was guilt by accompaniment.

Anyhoo we went to the game, had a good time, and then we had to come home. It was milking time 'bout then but when we got back to where we had left the mules, they were missing, yep; they had up and disappeared on us. Riding slowly up to the house, first thing we noticed Tom and Roadie were standing at the feed trough merrily munching on corn and switching their tails. They still had their harness on and two coal oil lanterns were hanging from their hames. Course Joann had to come bouncing from the smokehouse to inform us that we were dead or probably close to it.

I took that to mean Pa just wasn't very happy with us right about now. He never said a word, just pointed back down the road towards the crossing and the cornfield. Now my stomach was a flopping and growling, after all, I was a growing boy and dinner was long time gone. Joann also had to inform us Granny was having fried chicken for supper tonight and she'd be sure to eat ours for us. Man, my mouth was watering faster than I could swallow. I'm telling you, I was near starving to death. You know a growing boy needs nourishment to grow on.

Pay back was gonna be rough on the young lady, see in the winter that old dining room was as cold as an icicle. The steam would come off that food, if you wanted it warm when it went down your gizzard you had better eat fast. I mean when you talked, that is if you talked, you could see your own breath steaming out of your mouth. The old water bucket sitting there plumb full of drinking water would be froze solid every morning. Granny would always set it on the stove and thaw the poor thing out. Joann wouldn't go in there and sit down and eat, no sir, she'd beg us to bring her a biscuit and sausage or something, which kind and sweet as we were, we did. Uh huh, wait 'till this winter, the girl's gonna get awful hungry or she's gonna get awful cold, one or the other. You've heard the old saying, Remember the Alamo, well it's changed, now its Remember the Chicken.

Last thing I seen as the house passed from sight was Joann feeding the chickens with one of Granny's big sugar cookies sticking from her mouth. I could taste that cookie all the way to the field and I knew she knew it.

This time I didn't get to sit and chase a mole, no sir. I was out front with a lantern walking ahead of them contrary mules and wondering when they were gonna spook and run smack-dab over my poor little hungry body. Pa wanted those rows straight and RC had to be able to see to plow them straight. What a night, I was so hungry my stomach was pitching a fit. I do believe it was looking my liver over for a meal, and I was getting weak. Every time I'd ask about a rest, all I got from RC was a mean glare, and a gitup to the mules. I bet he was hungry too but he wouldn't complain or say a word if he starved to death, which I didn't figure was too far off. He was already awfully skinny; he sure didn't need to be missing any meals.

Well we finished the cornfield in time for breakfast and I mean just in the nick of time. Five more minutes and I knew I would perish right there, not having the strength to get back home. I knew Granny was feeling sorry for us, not Joann though, not a bit, she was still full of chicken. If I didn't miss my guess, we were still gonna get a hiding before the day was out, which we did. Leastways I went to the smokehouse on a full stomach. Now I knew why they always fed a condemned man before they hung him. Man I sure hated the thought of getting hung dead on an empty stomach.

Well the ball game had been a reprieve from work alright. One good thing that came out of it, we found out they were having horse racing the following Saturday at a flat track near Milburn. Now Pa traded for a bay mare that you couldn't turn in a fifty-acre field, that's why we called her Nail. When that mare was stretched out running, you couldn't turn her head or stop her until she just flat run down. I've seen RC put his foot in her neck, saw back on them reins, and that old mare would just stiff neck him and keep toting the mail. She could dang sure run a hole in the wind. There wasn't a thing on our place that could come close to beating her to the house when it came feeding time.

No one in the county knew we had her, or anything about the mare. Fact is we kinda kept her hid out, she weren't none to pretty, and she reminded me of Nita Faye Lowe. She wasn't the kind of horse that you'd want to ride to church on Sunday. No, not a soul knew of her, but RC with his little conniving ways was fixing to bring her to their attention quick, that is if I didn't miss my guess. That was after he got them to put down their money and wager against the old mare. Pa had mentioned at supper one night right after he bought her that someone at the sale barn said she was a thoroughbred, whatever that was.

Old Nail wasn't about to win a beauty contest that was sure but she was gentle enough for me to drive at my young innocent age. She would pull the light corn planter without a runaway, which is what kept her around the place. We made a good pair I reckon. We were both a little on the lazy side 'cept when it came to running. Now the only place I'd run to was the dinner table or after a coon. However, Old Nail loved to run and she was fast.

Pa didn't cotton to horseracing, no sir, shoot he didn't even like us trotting his teams to town on egg selling day. Anyway, the races were on Saturday and normally that was a bad day to try to slip away. Pa wasn't gonna Miss Nail, but RC was a frog of a different color. You ever counted the warts on a frog? Well RC was one wart Pa would miss and quick. This show was gonna be good, I could hardly wait to see how he was gonna pull this one off. I just got me one meeting with the razor strap and my backside wasn't in a hurry for another one. I didn't know how, when, or what reasoning he would try, but like I said, I wouldn't bet against the boy getting it done.

Race day arrived and believe it or not, RC wiggled his way out of working for the day. Pa and Granny, with Joann in tow were off to Milburn shopping. I figure Pa felt a mite guilty about working us poor young'uns. I had my choice, town or the horse races, my backside said town. I should have listened but man, I wanted to see them horses run. Surely, they were worth another meeting at the smokehouse. Pa was in a good mood as he started for town whistling his favorite tune not even looking back as he drove from sight with Granny sitting quietly beside him.

The little black mare and Nail were both lotted, something which should have tripped Pa's mind but I reckon he was preoccupied with town, cause he sure looked right straight at them before driving away. Now Pa was nobody's dummy, I already felt he knew about the races, shucks everybody else in the county did, so I figured he did to.

It didn't take long for us to get a halter on Nail and bridle the black mare and away we went. Charlie Dunn and Tim rode out on the road and met us at the crossroads, grinning from ear to ear. Kinda gave me goose bumps, them two sitting their horses grinning like a possum eating persimmons, yes sir made a body nervous for a fact.

Old Nail was a prancing and ringing her tail, the old gal's neck was bowed and her long skinny ears were jumping around like a pair of frog legs in a skillet. Yes sir, she were ready to run, the boys knew they were fixing to get rich. They all knew them dumb injuns would bet everything they owned against her. That was kinda funny, as the Dunn's were half Choctaw themselves.

We cut across the open fields staying away from the road just in case Pa had stopped to talk to a neighbor. We weren't worried about him showing up at the races, as he wouldn't waste his time going; at least I sure hoped he didn't. I done told myself if I seen head or hair of him, I was lighting a shuck out of there and quick. Those horses could find their own way back home.

The racetrack turned out to be just a straight away course, not an oval track like we heard. What a break, RC was fretting over how he was gonna get Nail to turn enough to follow the track. One thing was sure for certain, there were enough horses there to have the races. Every youngster in the country was present with their racehorse, chomping at the bits to get in on the fun. Course now I knew a lot of them nags and they couldn't out run a fat man on a hot day. I reckon some people have to learn the hard way.

Match races, relay races, and just plain old horse races were already set. RC left me sitting astride the black mare holding Nail as he walked over to enter the race. Charlie had entered his horse in the race just so he could get on the track and lead Nail to the starting line. Tim sat his horse at the end of the track ready to catch Nail as she passed, cause fact of the matter was, the old gal wasn't about to stop on her own.

I looked over the crowd and just knew our bacon was cooked. There was no way Pa wasn't gonna find out about this little escapade. It didn't matter that his horse would overnight become a bona fide racehorse, no siree bob, Pa was gonna kill us for sure. I gave considerable thought to just sneaking off and pleading innocent, but then RC would probably kill me. It was like the ant caught between a shoe and the ground, what we would call a rock and a hard place. Everyone at the races knew us;

someone would surely spill the beans. I warned RC, but the boy's mind was already made up, and he weren't about to change it. I'd found out a long time ago trying to change his mind was like trying to turn a runaway tornado, it wasn't gonna happen.

Old Nail, she was sure getting the horse laugh from most everybody causing RC to grin all the more. I didn't figure they'd be laughing much when this day was over. I admit she sure weren't much to look at from the front or side. That poor old mare had bones sticking out all over her, she definitely wasn't gonna win a beauty contest. Well pretty quick, unless I missed my guess, all they'd be seeing would be her backsides anyway.

There was so many horses that the races had to be run in rounds, then the winners would be brought back for the big finale. RC was finally called and Charlie led the high-strung mare to the starting line. I swear when that flag went down, and Charlie released Old Nail, RC practically landed behind the saddle as she tore out. Now the whole idea or plot was to keep her slowed down so the other riders didn't know exactly how fast she was. There was a lot of betting left and if she ran off and left the field behind eating dust, the bets would be finished. Trouble was how was RC gonna keep the mare back in the pack for just a few seconds? That's where Charlie and his horse came in to play. No one else seemed to notice, but Nail had her head pulled over to Charlie's saddle. He held the lead rope holding the old mare back from running.

She couldn't run away with that lead rope tied to her, no sir. The finish line was coming up fast so RC gave her a nudge. Charlie flipped him the rope letting Nail slip easily ahead of the others winning by a couple of lengths, heads or whatever. Anyway, she won but the race wasn't over yet. Tim setting at the finish line still had to catch the old idgit before she ran all the way home. With RC tugging on her and Tim whipping his horse for all it was worth, he finally managed to overtake her and get hold of her halter.

I won me a few marbles on the first race, then up and lost a few betting on a piece of crow bait that Leaky Aimes gave me a tip on. He foxed me for sure, that horse couldn't have outran me, anyway after I settled up my marble bet I tried my best to settle up with Leaky. I was coming out the loser on that deal too before some of the men broke up our disagreement. Course now there was always another day, if'n I'd had any sense I wouldn't have made that bet. It wasn't that I was a bad loser; well maybe it was. I just hated to lose, especially when the other feller snookered me and was laughing about it.

By the time RC was called up for the last race, I won me a few bets and was several marbles ahead, plus a black eye and a bloody nose. Well I had plenty of blood and the black eye would go away, so I figured I was way ahead.

RC came walking over and I knew right away he was up to no good when he collared me. Pointing over at where Leon Perkins stood waiting beside his horse, RC whispered his new plot in my ear. Sure enough, he done had another scheme on his mind. Old Leon had the champion racehorse from last year's races so he sure wasn't worried about his horse Blackjack losing to our bag of bones. Now I normally wasn't eager to get in on RC's schemes but this time I was more than willing. Seems like several years earlier at a Christmas Party, when I was still real small, Mister Leon Perkins flipped a lit cigarette butt down my britches. Man you talk about yelling and doing a jig, the older boys thought that was downright funny at least until my mother got her hands on them.

Like I said, I was willing and eager, so I wandered over to where Leon stood talking to some of his cronies. I didn't like any of them all too much, but as I didn't reach but a little higher than their belt buckles there wasn't much I could do about it just yet. I knew Leon or one of them smart alecks would badger me into a bet so I played my part to the hilt. I was acting real innocent like when I told them boys I wouldn't bet a dime or a marble on the old horse, as she was wind broke and probably couldn't make it through this race let alone another one. Old Leon's ears perked up like a hoot owls sitting on a limb when he was watching a chicken coop. Yes sir, I had him hook, line, and sinker. A poor dumb looking little kid like me was too stupid to lie about a thing like that. He already forgot about the cigarette butt but my rear end hadn't, it still had the scar and would probably carry it for life. Yep I was branded like one of Pa's cows.

Sure enough, Leon sent one of his sidekicks to hit RC up about a bet. I had to admit RC looked like one of those actor fellers in the movies we got to see a time or two. He was a shaking his head doubtfully, shrugging his shoulders and playing downright dumb, that was before he slammed shut the trap. The bet was on; I even got some more marbles down on the old girl.

The race turned out to be a little difficult this time. RC didn't have Charlie to hold the mare so they had to try to hold her afoot. Now that was a mistake, that mare might have been skinny and ugly, but she was stout and could act a fool when she wanted to. Old Charlie was trying his best to hold her, but was getting the worst of it when the flag went down and them seven horses tore out with Nail bringing up the rear. Charlie was still dusting himself off when the horses crossed the finish line with Nail again barely winning by a nose.

Old Leon was fit to be tied, hollering foul, hollering cheat, or just plain hollering. His black horse Blackjack had just barely lost and he yelled his horse had been shouldered aside at the finish line. Course RC was apologizing, but insisted he was innocent. He offered Leon another race so he could have a chance of getting his money back. Well, sure enough Leon he fell for it and another wager was made. RC won some serious money already. I was hoping he would call it a day before something bad happened, like Pa finding out we were at the horse races running poor old Nail.

About that time, I watched the betting money land smack-dab in the beefy hands of the man judging the races. I knew for a fact, the fat was in the fire. The final race was on; this time there would only be two horses in the race. What folks called a matched race, between Old Nail and Leon Perkins' Blackjack Horse.

Leon listened to my story and swallowed it like a worm down a bird's mouth. He figured with stretching the mare out a little she would run out of steam and lose the next race for sure. To my surprise, the mare was standing at the starting line just as quiet as a church mouse. She'd done run two races so I figured she had run some of the starch out of herself. I just hoped she had another good race in her. I had bet almost every marble I owned on this last race. If Nail lost, I'd be out of the marble playing business for quite a spell.

The starting flag was flying in the breeze; Old Nail was just standing there almost asleep, kinda like she did me when we were planting corn. I was a little worried hoping she was planning on waking up. RC grabbed himself a good handful of mane and leaned forward as that flag fell. Well sir, when that flag dropped and RC kicked poor old Nail, my teeth almost fell out on the ground.

That mare left there like a six-legged ape and I mean to tell you she was turning on the speed. Poor old Blackjack looked like he was standing still the way she was leaving him in the dust. Well it didn't take much figuring on who was fixing to win this race, the boys I had bet with just handed over their marbles and walked off shaking their heads. I was rich; my pockets were so full of marbles I couldn't get on the black mare's back. Old Leon passed by on his black horse and frowned down at me, kinda mad like. I just had to grin and pat my backside, I couldn't help myself. You know, payback is sure rough some times.

I sounded like a can of rocks rolling down a hill when I rode away. I was grinning from ear to ear just before I seen Tim and Charlie riding back to where I was waiting. They were empty handed, no Nail, which meant no RC. Tim filled me in on the fact the mare had eluded him and the last he seen of her she was headed for home with RC hollering whoa every ten jumps. Now if you picture it in your head it's kinda funny sounding. It seems when RC turned on our road still hollering whoa to the runaway Nail, who was just beginning to get wound out, guess who was a quarter mile ahead of him? Yep, you guessed it, Pa and Granny were leisurely headed for home all smiles and having the time of their lives. Well they were before Old Nail flew by them a mile a minute and started them mules to trying to run. I reckon that old mare had done all the racing she wanted for the day, she was headed to the farm for her supper and she was toting the mail.

RC didn't stop shucks he couldn't but he said he could hear Pa a cussing them mules and hollering whoa all the way down the road. I guess me and the Dunn's boys missed out on the fun, but I'm mighty glad I was late getting in for the supper chores that evening. Sure was gonna be interesting watching RC wiggle out of this one. For once, I was nowhere to be seen and I could plead complete innocence.

Anyway, I wound up with over a hundred marbles, a black eye, and a bloody nose for the day, can't say for sure how much RC won. Charlie collected the money from Leon who was cussing with every breath he took. Funny thing was, you know Pa never said a word about the races. No sir, he never mentioned it at all. I reckon he was remembering the raft betting at Wilsons and figured RC hadn't done any different than he had.

RC would always smile when he held up that big wad of money he came into. Me, I'd rather have the marbles, a boy sure can't shoot dollar bills. Old Delmar and me still had our differences to settle but after the races, I was up on him for quite a few marbles. Sad thing about the whole deal was Old Nail, bless her ugly little self, she done all the work, but me and RC got all the marbles and the money.

There are lots of stories about Old Rover but these are the ones I remember with the fondest memories. He was without a doubt the smartest, most loyal dog I ever knew. Go down to Blue Crossing and stand on the sandy banks of Blue River. Listen real hard; somewhere off in the distance you'll hear'em. Rover, Quane, Fanny, and Rock, they'll be running a hot coon track, bawling all the way and letting you hear the pretty music. Folks, Carl Dennis wasn't rich in money, but he was rich, he had an abundance of love from his family, respect from his friends and neighbors, and he had Rover. Like he said, that's all a man could wish for out of life.

The End

www.ingramcontent.com/pod-product-compliance
Lightning Source LLC
Chambersburg PA
CBHW072129020426

42334CB00018B/1720